M000309086

Reflections for New Mothers

Ellen Sue Stern

Meadowbrook Press

Distributed by Simon & Schuster
New York

Library of Congress Cataloging-in-Publication Data
Stern, Ellen Sue, 1954-
    Reflections for new mothers : 365 daily meditations /
    by Ellen Sue Stern.
        p. cm.
    ISBN 0-88166-398-0 (Meadowbrook) --
    ISBN 0-7432-3450-2 (Simon & Schuster)
        1. Mothers—Prayer-books and devotions—English.
        2. Motherhood—Religious aspects—Christianity—Meditations.
        3. Devotional calendars. I. Title.
    BV4847 .S74 2002
    306.874'3--dc21

                                                    2002003407

Editorial Director: Christine Zuchora-Walske
Editor and Contributing Writer: Angela Wiechmann
Proofreader: Megan McGinnis
Desktop Publishing: Heather Kern, Peggy Bates
Production Manager: Paul Woods
Cover Art: Melanie Marder Parks

© 2002 by Ellen Sue Stern

Published by Meadowbrook Press, 5451 Smetana Drive, Minnetonka,
Minnesota 55343

www.meadowbrookpress.com

BOOK TRADE DISTRIBUTION by Simon and Schuster, a division of
Simon and Schuster, Inc., 1230 Avenue of the Americas, New York,
New York 10020

06 05 04 03 02   10 9 8 7 6 5 4 3 2 1

Printed in the United States of America

BIRTH DAY

Oh, baby. Come closer. Eye to eye, soul to soul.
Come say hello to your new-born mother.
                                                          —*Phyllis Chesler*

Welcome! Welcome to your baby! Welcome
to motherhood!

For nearly a year you have anticipated meeting
your child. Now the day has finally arrived. As you
hold your baby in your arms, look with joy, with
gratitude for having reached this wondrous
moment. Share your fears, hopes, and dreams for
the future.

You have so much to look forward to, so much
to learn, so much to do as you begin your new
life together.

This is indeed a new day. A day of celebration.
A fleeting, unforgettable time when newborn and
mother finally meet.

Affirmation: I celebrate the beginning of a new life.

THE FIRST CRY

*Your baby's first cry is the one you hear in
the delivery room, the triumphant, tension-
shattering sound that says, "I'm here, I'm
breathing, I'm alive!"*

—Katherine Karlsrud

Thank God! That first wonderful cry!

Never before was the sound of a cry so heartily
welcomed, so deeply reassuring. No matter how
many times you heed your child's cry and soothe
him in the years to come, no cry will ever hold so
much promise and so much pleasure as that first
cry in the delivery room.

You carried and nurtured your child for nine
months inside you. You labored to bring him into
this world. Now he's here, no longer a part of you
but a separate being, announcing his arrival with a
triumphant cry.

Affirmation: Thank heavens for that first cry.

CUTTING THE CORD

The broken cord may yet be joined again
But in the midst a knot will remain.

—*Anwari-I sueill*

The symbolism of cutting the umbilical cord is powerful, poignant. After nine months, you've reached the moment of separation, of cutting loose, of accepting your child's entrance into the world as an independent individual.

Yet the cord is never completely severed. You feel the tug when your baby cries inconsolably and you would do anything to take away the pain. You'll someday feel the knot of motherhood when your child turns to you and says, "I hurt, Mommy. Fix it."

My children—Evan, eighteen, and Zoe, twenty—date, ride off in their cars, and go away to school. Yet there are moments when they curl back into my arms, almost as if to reconnect the cord. We are forever tied.

Affirmation: The mother-child knot is forever.

FEAR

*I remember leaving the hospital...thinking, "Wait,
are they going to let me just walk off with him?
I don't know beans about babies!"*

—Anne Tyler

That's exactly how I felt after Zoe was born. I had
never fed or diapered a baby before, never even
held one for longer than two minutes; the idea of
being totally responsible for her was nothing short
of terrifying.

It's a bit of a shock when it sinks in that the
baby is actually yours and definitely here to stay.
It's scary, especially when you acknowledge how
fragile and dependent your baby is.

Here's what I discovered: Those first twenty-
four hours are trial by fire. At 4:00 A.M., when
the baby's screaming to be fed ("Didn't we just
feed her? Oh, I'm too tired to remember!") and
you're fumbling in the dark for a diaper, you
figure out really fast what to do and how to do it.

Contrary to myth, mothering isn't wholly
instinctive. Every new mother learns as she goes.
With each passing day, you'll become more and
more comfortable.

Affirmation: This is trial by fire, and I'll learn as I go.

NIGHT FEEDINGS

I actually remember feeling delight, at two o'clock in the morning, when the baby woke for his feed, because I so longed to have another look at him.

—Margaret Drabble

In my Expecting Change workshops, pregnant women explore the emotional changes of pregnancy. In one exercise, I guide participants as they visualize their perfect fantasy of the first twenty-four hours at home with their babies.

Interestingly, few expectant mothers fantasize about sleeping through the night. In almost every case, the great majority looks forward to the middle-of-the-night feedings as precious time with their newborns.

I can easily understand why. Although sleep is at a premium, there's something incredibly intimate about those middle-of-the-night moments—sitting in utter silence, rocking and cuddling as moonlight streams through the window. Few moments with your child are as peaceful and as sweet.

Affirmation: I'll savor these late-night feedings.

WEIGHT LOSS

*I was so thankful not to be pregnant any more,
I laughed and stroked my body which now only
belonged to me once again.*

—Jane Lazarre

What an amazing feeling to slowly rub your hand
over your flat tummy. (Well, at least it's flat by
comparison.) You'll be able to lie on your
stomach, bend over to tie your shoes, and
gradually ease back into your old jeans.

The operative word here is *gradually*. Although
most women experience a significant weight drop
following delivery, losing those last ten or fifteen
pounds can be excruciatingly slow. Don't be disappointed if your stomach looks like crepe paper
or if you can only fit into your early maternity
clothes. With a healthy diet, exercise, and time,
the extra weight will eventually disappear.

Be easy on yourself. It took nine months for
your baby to grow. Give yourself at least that
much time to get back in shape.

Affirmation: I'll be patient as my body recovers.

SENSUOUSNESS

*The world has never felt or looked, sounded,
smelled or tasted so wonderful as it does today!*
—*Sandra Drescher-Lehman*

Your baby is a highly sensuous being from the
moment of birth. He likes to look in your eyes. He
recognizes your voice. He enjoys being massaged
and held close. He likes sweet flavors and the
smell of your milk.

Your baby's senses allow him to discover the
world, discover you and your partner, and
discover himself.

Knowing that your baby is so sensuous makes
you, too, feel more in tune with your senses.
Colors seem brighter, caresses seem more tender,
flavors seem fuller, music seems more resonant,
aromas seem more fragrant.

In these first few days, your baby will discover
a magical, sensuous new world, and so will you.

Affirmation: My baby and I are sensuous.

HIGH-RISK BABIES

*'Tis better to have loved and lost
than never to have loved at all.*
—*Alfred Tennyson*

Some parents of high-risk babies withhold their love subconsciously, fearing that bonding with the babies, only to lose them, would be unbearable.

But when there's a chance to love—even at the risk of losing that love—you mustn't pass it up.

If your baby was born with a life-threatening medical condition, have faith that this tiny, fragile being possesses the strength to survive. Have hope that you'll soon take her home and that she'll live a long, happy life. But most of all, love your baby with your whole heart. Don't hold back. Your love may give your little one the extra courage to hold on for dear life.

Affirmation: I'll love my baby at all costs.

CHILDBIRTH

I think of my children's births—carry them around with me every day of my life.

—Joyce Maynard

Not many days ago, you were carefully breathing, timing contractions, and pushing with every ounce of strength and stamina to complete the marathon of a lifetime: the birth of your baby.

Now that the baby's here, your attention is focused elsewhere. Time goes by in a blur of sleepless nights and endless changing, feeding, and burping. Your baby's birth fades into the background. It begins to seem like a remote dreamscape (or awful nightmare, depending on how things went).

It's important to hold on to your birth experience and commit it to a special place in your memory. The same courage you summoned during childbirth will serve you well as you meet the staggering challenges of motherhood. Take a moment now to recall how it felt to give birth to your child. Remember your pain, your joy, your triumph.

Affirmation: I'll always remember what it took to give birth to my child.

MOOD SWINGS

*She remembered it as a time of intense feeling,
the days when their child had just been born.*
—Barbara Einzig

All your emotions are amplified in the first days
and weeks postpartum. One moment you're filled
with the greatest joy you've ever experienced.
The next second, you're weeping for no apparent
reason. Both happiness and sadness are more
intense, and you often shift back and forth
between the emotions so fast that you can't
figure out what's happening.

So what *is* happening?

It's a combination of hormones, fatigue, and
the sheer emotional shock of suddenly having a
brand-new human being in your care. No wonder
you're ecstatic, exhausted, and overwhelmed at
the same time.

Let yourself laugh. Let yourself cry as much as
you need to. You're not going crazy; you're not
suffering from postpartum psychosis. You're
simply responding to the powerfully dramatic
transition from pregnancy to motherhood.

**Affirmation: My postpartum emotions are normal
and natural.**

CHECKUPS

Some hospitals provide a clinic visit or home visit by one of their nurses to check on you and the baby, to answer questions, and to offer practical advice.

*—Penny Simkin, Janet Whalley,
and Ann Keppler*

When the health aide called at nine in the morning and asked if I wanted her to make a visit, I was wearily sterilizing bottles, staring at last night's dinner dishes in the sink, and wearing the same soiled sweat suit I'd fallen asleep in. The only thing I wanted was someone to take my brand-new baby off my hands so I could temporarily escape.

Of course, that's not what the checkup is for. But if you have questions, concerns, or problems, especially of a medical nature, or if you simply want reassurance, it's great to have an on-call resource to turn to. The nurse won't baby-sit for you, but this checkup may help you ease into these first few days of motherhood.

Affirmation: The checkup will be helpful (even if the nurse can't baby-sit).

BONDING

I did not feel anything like the warm bond I was supposed to feel for this bundle newly removed from my body.

—Angela Barron McBride

Bonding. That nebulous, all-important attachment you're "supposed" to feel the instant your child is born.

Some women bond immediately with their babies. For others, it takes hours, days, even weeks or months until they feel unequivocally enchanted with their babies.

How quickly you bond depends on lots of things: your birth experience, nursing, your child's gender, along with any number of personal emotional factors. But whether you bond immediately or over time has nothing to do with how much you love your child. I bonded with Zoe on the spot; it took longer with Evan, yet I grew to adore him every bit as much.

In the end, what is known as "bonding" doesn't have to happen in the first instant you meet your baby. As in any important relationship, real intimacy between mother and child takes time.

Affirmation: We have years and years to bond.

GRATITUDE

*We never know the love of our parents for us till
we have become parents.*

—Henry Ward Beecher

I remember sitting bleary-eyed in the rocking chair
shortly after Zoe's birth, feeding her at 4:30 A.M.
and thinking to myself, "My mother got up in the
middle of the night just like this with me."

Having a child makes your appreciation for
your own parents soar. You realize how much
they sacrificed to make a home, to provide the
necessities—let alone the luxuries. You understand
their fears, their struggles, the countless ways they
set aside their needs to provide for yours. And
you realize how much they must have loved you.

As you gaze upon your child, feeling intense
love and devotion, you think of your parents with
newfound gratitude and respect.

**Affirmation: Now I understand what my parents
did for me.**

PATERNITY LEAVE

Studies show that when a father is involved with his child's care from birth, he continues to be involved in the child's life as she grows up.
                    —Glade B. Curtis and Judith Schuler

The average new father takes a few days off from work immediately after the baby is born, but then returns to his usual nine-to-five routine. In some cases, his return to work is a financial necessity. In other cases, it may be because the father simply hasn't considered taking paternity leave.

If your partner can take paternity leave, he can help you recuperate from childbirth. He can offer support as a full-time on-site parent, and together you can ease into parenthood. Perhaps most im–portantly, paternity leave will give your partner time to develop a deep and lasting bond with your child.

Paternity leave is an attractive option for most families; unfortunately, it's a realistic option for few. Evaluate your situation and see if paternity leave is possible for your partner. It's a wonderful way to begin his life as a father and your life as a family.

Affirmation: Paternity leave is an option to consider.

INTIMACY

*In the sheltered simplicity of the first days after a
baby is born, one sees again the magical closed
circle...of two people existing only for each other.*
—Anne Morrow Lindbergh

The intimacy between mother and child goes
way beyond closeness, beyond comfort, beyond
caring. It's a connection so infinite, so impene-
trable, you sometimes forget anyone or anything
else exists.

It's a connection so infinite, so impene-
In the first weeks of motherhood, make sure to
give yourself lots of time alone with your baby—
time to rock and cuddle, time to count fingers and
toes over and over, time for just the two of you to
be wrapped up in your own little world.

It's also important to open the circle to others,
especially your partner. Relish the sweet and
magical intimacy between you and your child, but
also be sure your partner, older children, extended
family, and friends bond with the baby and give
you the nurturing companionship you need.

**Affirmation: This is a magical time for my baby
and me.**

EMPTINESS

But now I feel empty. My secret is gone.
                    —Sandra Drescher-Lehman

During these first few days, you may feel strangely empty.

After all, for nine months your baby grew inside you, pushing and prodding and stretching your body in ways you never thought imaginable. For nine months, you protected the little life inside you, kept it warm, nourished, safe. The beautiful intimacy filled your whole body and soul.

And now it's gone, and you can't help but feel empty.

Don't worry. Your love for your baby and the joy of motherhood will fill the emptiness and make you whole again.

Affirmation: Joy and love will fill my emptiness.

MYSTERY

When you bring Baby home from the hospital, he seems like a beloved stranger, a tiny mystery.
—Babies, Bottles, and Booties

Although you've "known" your baby since conception, now that he's here in the flesh, you may feel as if you've invited a stranger into your home, a mystery into your life. You don't know his personality, likes, dislikes, needs, dreams, fears, or wants. You don't know a single thing about him.

How do you get to know this little stranger? How do you solve this tiny mystery cloaked in diapers and blankets?

The key to unlocking the mystery is time. Each minute you spend with your baby, you learn more about him. Over the coming days, weeks, months, and years, you'll get to know him better and better.

Affirmation: My baby won't remain a stranger for long.

BODY

Try not to inspect your wife's episiotomy stitches. Sure, you'll get over it if you look, but if you're like me, you just don't need this in your memory bank.

—James Douglas Barron

Yes, your partner's amazed by what your body accomplished. But he may be a little uneasy about the garish stitches holding your tender parts together. And he may be put off by the fact that you're constantly leaking from all the parts he associates with lovemaking.

If your partner feels this way, don't give him a guilt trip or get angry. You probably have similar feelings. Reassure him that although your body has endured some changes, it still belongs to the same woman he's always loved and found so sexy.

Affirmation: Let's talk about the changes my body has endured.

HOPE

Bringing a child into the world is the greatest act of hoping there is.

—Louise Hart

As all new mothers know, having a baby requires hope.

You hope the pregnancy goes well, and you hope childbirth goes smoothly. You hope the baby won't cry too much, and you hope you'll quickly learn how to feed, diaper, and soothe her. You hope she'll sleep through the night—or at least long enough so you don't look like a zombie from *Night of the Living Dead* the next morning.

More than anything, you hope you'll be a good parent. You hope your child will be a good person. You hope your relationship with your partner will survive or, better yet, flourish. You hope your family will be filled with love.

Hold your hopes as dearly as you hold your baby. Your hope will see you through.

Affirmation: I hope _____

_____.

EMOTIONS

There aren't words yet invented to define the emotions a mother feels as she cuddles her newborn child.

—Janet Leigh

Awed. Overwhelmed. Flooded with tenderness that you never imagined.

None of these words entirely describes the waves of emotion you feel as you cradle your baby in your arms. Such deep and boundless love. Such passionate commitment. And so much at stake.

Although you may tell your child how much you love him every day for the rest of your life, it's impossible to convey completely the pure emotional intensity experienced in the early weeks of motherhood.

Invest in a journal and try to express your feelings now, while they're fresh. Or write a letter to your child, one that will serve as a keepsake of the first precious days of your life together.

Affirmation: I love you more than words can say.

FATHERS

Babies don't need fathers, but mothers do. Someone who is taking care of a baby needs to be taken care of.

—*Amy Heckerling*

The first part of this quote is questionable. I'd argue that, with the obvious exception of nursing, babies need fathers just as much as they need mothers. However, the second half of this quote is right on the money. Especially in the first several months of a child's life, mothers need to be mothered.

Newborns are incredibly hard work! There's constant maintenance and nonstop nurturing, and when the baby finally takes a nap, you want to nap, too, but there's loads of laundry to do and piles of toys to pick up.

You need loving, and lots of it. If not by the baby's father, by someone—a friend or a parent—who can replenish the energy continually pouring out of you. You need cuddling, massages, good food, and tons of support and encouragement.

At this stage of motherhood, your baby's not the only one who needs to be "babied."

Affirmation: I'll let myself be nurtured.

A DAY IN THE LIFE

You eagerly awaited a natural, joyful birthing experience. But complications arose, causing you to have a C-section. It was a terrible disappointment, and you can't help but feel like a failure.

Take your baby in your arms right now. Hold her closely, watching her tiny chest rise and fall with each delicate breath. Now ask yourself, "Was childbirth a failure?"

Of course it wasn't. No matter what you hoped it would be and no matter what the circumstances were, childbirth was a success because you're now a mother with a baby to love.

Childbirth is a momentous event—one that inspires nine months of hopes, dreams, fears, and worries—but it doesn't determine your worth as a woman and a mother. How you bring your baby into the world is insignificant when compared to how you love and raise her once she's born.

Affirmation: Childbirth was a success!

SMILES

When you are drawing up your list of life's miracles, you might place near the top of the list the first moment your baby smiles at you.

—*Bob Greene*

Some say it's just gas or a reflex. Don't believe it for a minute!

Whatever its origins, it's an amazing moment when your baby's face first lights up in a smile. When his face crinkles up and breaks into that inimitable grin, all the sacrifices are suddenly worthwhile. It's a reward for all the sleepless nights and all the dirty diapers. It feels wonderful to know that your baby's happy and content.

When your baby smiles, you smile. In fact, everything in the room seems to smile from the beauty and light radiating from your child.

Affirmation: What a smile!

AGE

Lord, be with me—
I've come late to the dance.

—*Sharon Hudnell*

These poignant words come from "Delayed
Motherhood Waltz," a poem about a mother
who has a baby later in life.

Although experts suggest women should
have babies between the ages of twenty and
thirty-five, more and more women over thirty-five
are becoming mothers. This may be because of
voluntary reasons (such as desire to concentrate
on career, education, or independence) or in-
voluntary reasons (such as infertility, lack of a
partner, or lack of financial stability).

If you're a new mother who's over thirty-five,
you may feel as if you've come late to the dance.
Actually, you're just on time. Your age makes no
difference to your baby and doesn't limit your
ability to be a good mother.

**Affirmation: No matter how old I am, I can be
a good mother.**

AGE

When I was pregnant with Meredith, I was nine-teen…. I remember thinking, What kind of a life could I give her?

—*Ellen Waller*

Most new mothers have moments when they feel insecure about caring for their babies. Teenage mothers may feel nearly crippled by insecurity.

In a sense, teenagers are in a second infancy. They take their first steps of independence from their parents, and they learn who they are and how the world works. It's no wonder then that some teen mothers doubt their ability to care for their babies. They barely feel able to care for themselves, let alone for dependent babies.

If you're a teen mother, don't be ashamed of your self-doubt—it's perfectly natural. Nev–ertheless, trust in your love for your baby. Get support from the father of the baby, if possible, and from your family and friends. Take comfort in the fact that your baby doesn't care about your age. She loves you deeply and completely because you're her mother.

Affirmation: No matter how young I am, I can be a good mother.

A DAY IN THE LIFE

Your mother stops by to visit. First she comments that the baby must be cold wearing only a diaper and undershirt, then she questions how long you plan to nurse, then she demonstrates a better way to burp him. You're getting annoyed. In fact, you wish she'd disappear!

For centuries, mothers have given their daughters parenting advice, especially when the babies are new and the daughters are learning the basics. To whatever degree possible, don't let your mother's advice unnerve you. It won't do you any good to throw out the mother with the maternity advice.

Try saying calmly, "Thanks for your help, Mom, but it's important for me to make my own decisions regarding my baby." Let her know you appreciate her concern, and maybe take her comments into consideration. After all, she may know something you don't, and even if her advice is outdated, it won't hurt you to listen.

If possible, be assertive without being aggressive so you can both enjoy your new relationships as mother and grandmother.

Affirmation: I'll gently assert myself with my mother.

DIAPERS

All sorts of cool movie stars bragged about using washable diapers, so my wife and I decided to give them a whirl.

—James Douglas Barron

Choosing between disposable and washable diapers isn't as easy as choosing between paper and plastic bags at the grocery store. Your needs as a parent may not dovetail with your beliefs as an environmentalist.

Washable diapers are better for the environment, but they take a lot of work to clean. They're cheaper than disposables, but not if you can't sanitize them properly at home and must hire a diaper service.

Disposables are more convenient and can often handle a bigger "load," but they're quickly piling up in landfills.

You need to weigh the pros and cons of each type of diaper and make the best decision possible. Whatever you feel most comfortable with will be the right choice.

Affirmation: I'll carefully choose what kind of diapers my baby uses.

JEALOUSY

*Pregnant women! [T]hey had that preciousness
which they imposed wherever they went,
compelling attention, constantly reminding you
that they carried the future inside.*

—Ruth Morgan

When you were pregnant, people looked at you
with a certain amount of awe. The attention made
you feel special, magical, and beautiful. But now
that you've given birth, the attention has shifted.
People have eyes only for the baby.

It's natural to feel envious of your baby. Don't
be ashamed. After nine months of pregnancy and
all its magic, you've been swept into motherhood
and all its harsh realities. It'll take time to adjust to
your new role.

For now, don't be afraid to ask for more
support if you feel your needs aren't being met.
And as you gaze upon your baby, realize that just
as the two of you shared the attention for the first
nine months, you can certainly share it now.

**Affirmation: I'll adjust to getting less attention
than I got during pregnancy.**

DELIVERANCE

*So just keep on letting go, 'cause I must be close
to being delivered for the first time.*

—Jakob Dylan

During childbirth, there came a moment when
you let go, when you surrendered. In that
moment, you delivered two people into this
world. You delivered your baby and, just as
importantly, yourself.

You've been delivered into motherhood,
a world full of emotions unlike any you've ever
experienced. You've been delivered into a new
identity that gives your life purpose, focus,
and meaning.

Let go of your old life. You can't turn back
now, nor would you want to.

**Affirmation: I've been delivered into a new life
of motherhood.**

IN-LAWS

It's no problem to hand my baby to my parents,
but I have a hard time handing her to my in-laws.
—New Mother

New mothers are often protective of their babies;
some don't feel comfortable handing them to
anyone but their partners and their trusted
relatives and friends. This may explain why some
mothers are reluctant to let the in-laws bond with
the babies.

Even if you're not close with your in-laws, it's
important for them to bond with their grandchild.
The baby's as much a part of your partner as you,
and she's as much a part of your in-laws as your
parents. Let this be a time of closeness and
bonding for the entire family.

**Affirmation: I'll encourage my in-laws to bond
with the baby.**

NAMES

*The name we give to something shapes our
attitude toward it.*

—Katherine Paterson

During pregnancy, you probably spent a lot of
time poring over baby-name books and imagining
which name would fit your unborn baby. Now
that your baby has arrived and there's a name
on the birth certificate, how does the name fit?

If the name fits your baby perfectly, count
yourself lucky. But if calling your baby by the
name you loved during pregnancy now makes
you cringe, don't despair. Who says you can't
shorten his name? Who says you can't use his
middle name? Who says you can't use his initials?
Who says you can't call him Pumpkin, Monkey
Shine, or Munchkin?

You're not bound by any law to call your child
by the name on his birth certificate. Over the years,
your baby may grow into the formal name; but
for now, call him something that fits him perfectly.

**Affirmation: I'll call my baby by a name that fits—
not necessarily by the name on the birth certificate.**

A DAY IN THE LIFE

It's 11:00 A.M., and the baby finally went down for a nap. You were up four times during the night and are ready to collapse. The doorbell rings; it's your neighbor who threw you a baby shower. She's stopped by to visit. What do you do?

Thank her for coming, but tell her you'll give her a call when the baby's up.

Although it's hard to close the door in someone's face, it's imperative that you don't waste your precious R-and-R time visiting. Unless your neighbor has stopped by to stock the refrigerator or throw in three loads of laundry, in which case you can lie down while she does it, be firm about visiting hours. And even if your neighbor threw you the best baby shower in recorded history, never wake a sleeping baby if you can help it.

If this sounds selfish or rude, remember: Your neighbor can sleep soundly through the night. You need to replenish your energy for the next round—just a few short minutes ahead.

Affirmation: I'll be firm about visiting hours.

A DAY IN THE LIFE

You used to have a life. You had friends.
Interests. The ability to carry on an intelligent
conversation. Now you walk around in a daze.
You haven't slept, read a newspaper, or been
anywhere other than the 7-Eleven and the
pediatrician's office for a week. You're starting to
wonder, "When will my life get back to normal?"

This *is* normal. At least for the next few months,
you may as well resign yourself to the fact that
your life has changed. It's mind-boggling, I know.
You wanted a baby, but you didn't want the end
of life as you knew it.

Here are the guidelines for sanity: In the first
three months, don't expect *anything* of yourself
other than doing your best to care for your baby.
In months four through six, gradually return to
your job or your other activities. By then, you'll
be amazed at how much your quality of life
has improved.

Affirmation: This is my life.

COLIC

The colic makes me feel like a shitty mother, not to mention impotent and lost and nuts.
—Anne Lamont

There's really no medical explanation for colic. There's no ready routine or remedy to prevent a colic outburst or successfully stop it. In other words, there's really nothing you can do if you have a colicky baby—except live with it.

Dealing with colic floods you with frustration, helplessness, and hopelessness because no matter how hard you try, you can't change the situation.

But what can change is your attitude. You have the power to set your negative feelings aside and focus instead on feelings of compassion, strength, and hope. Repeat to yourself: "I have the compassion to care for my child in this difficult time. I have the strength to survive whatever life deals me. I have the hope that someday this will end."

Affirmation: I can't change my colicky baby, but I can change my attitude.

TWINS

*There are two things in this life for which we are
never fully prepared and that is—twins.*
—Josh Billings

For a mother of twins, life is often like the
Doublemint gum slogan: "Double your pleasure,
double your fun." But stress, exhaustion, and
work are doubled, too.

If you have twins, your first goal is to master
the basics as best as you can. Caring for two
babies is an extreme challenge. Get as much
support as you can. Your partner needs to be an
equal parent, but you also may need a few other
people to help occasionally with such things as
meals, housework, and baby-sitting.

It may take you some time, but you'll soon
have the basics under control. Your next goal will
then be to let yourself experience the joy, love,
and happiness that doubles the moment two
babies enter your life.

**Affirmation: Twins are double the work, double
the joy.**

PLANNING

*We want far better reasons for having children
than not knowing how to prevent them.*
—Dora Russell

Some women plan to have children, controlling all
the details right down to the due date. They seem
to be completely prepared for motherhood, ready
to take on all its challenges.

But if your pregnancy came as a surprise—
pleasant or otherwise—you may be overwhelmed.
You weren't able to wait until you got the promotion, until the car was paid off, or until you
bought a house. More importantly, you weren't
able to make the conscious decision to become a
mother. You may feel unprepared and therefore
incapable of being a good parent.

The truth is, no one can be completely
prepared to be a mother. Whether you spent
a year organizing every aspect of your life in
anticipation of a baby or whether you were one
of the statistical few whose birth control failed,
your love for your baby and your desire to learn
will make you a good mother.

**Affirmation: Regardless of whether I planned to
have this baby, I'll be a good mother.**

FEAR

*I dream of your sudden death. The stopped breath.
The violent choking. The mysterious convulsion.*
—Phyllis Chesler

During these first few months, it's natural to be
hypervigilant. Fears of crib death bring you to
your baby's side at all hours of the day and night.
You study her complexion and count her breaths.

It's a way of coming to terms with how
incredibly fragile your child is and how awesome
the responsibility for her care is. It's simply a
sign of how deeply you love her and how
unimaginably heartbroken you would be to lose
what you can barely believe is yours.

You may want to resist the urge to climb in the
crib, but there's no reason not to stand by it until
you're absolutely reassured. As the weeks go by,
you'll rest easier, knowing that your baby is okay.

**Affirmation: My fear is a natural expression of
my love.**

SUPPORT

*The women of the Samois tribe bring meals to the
new mother for the first month following birth.*
—*Anonymous*

In many cultures, mothers are cared for following
the births of babies. Members of the community
clean the home, massage the new mother, and
bring her food so she can recover and focus her
attention on her baby.

Unfortunately, in urban North America, most
new moms are left virtually alone to cope with the
physical and emotional adjustments postpartum.
Since North American culture doesn't offer strong
community support, it's natural for new moms to
feel isolated and depleted. It's up to you to create
whatever support you can for yourself. Ask
neighbors, friends, and family to deliver food,
help with laundry, and do any other tasks that
can lighten your load.

**Affirmation: I'll ask for and accept as much help
as possible.**

PARENTING STYLES

*How to fold a diaper depends on the size of the
baby and the diaper.*

—Benjamin Spock

And how to cradle an infant depends on the
size of the infant and your arms. And how to
discipline a toddler depends on the size of the
toddler and the problem. And how to answer a
child's question depends on the size of the child
and the question.

Dr. Spock's advice is applicable to every stage
of parenting. There's no one way to parent; it
all depends on the magnitude of the challenge
and the dimensions—physical and emotional—
of the child.

Knowing that there's no one way to parent is
both a relief and a challenge.

**Affirmation: There are many different ways
to parent.**

A DAY IN THE LIFE

You've been a bundle of mixed emotions during this first month, but much to your surprise, so has your partner. He's riding as many highs and lows as you are, but he doesn't have any hormones raging through his body. What's the deal?

Baby blues aren't completely hormonal and therefore limited to mothers. New fathers can have bouts of postpartum blues, too.

It shouldn't be too hard to understand why your partner has such mood swings. Just like you, he's had his life turned upside down by this new baby. Like you, he's probably as frightened as he is delighted. If he's taking on an equal share of parenting, he's struggling to learn how to care for a demanding baby. And although his body didn't experience childbirth, he, too, is fatigued, sleep-deprived, and running on pure adrenaline these days—especially if he's working full-time outside the home.

Don't dismiss your partner's postpartum blues. Give him the same love and support you want him to give you during this difficult time.

Affirmation: My partner can get baby blues, too.

SOUNDS

Run the vacuum, turn on the radio to static, run water, play nature sounds, run the washing machine or dishwasher.
—*Glade B. Curtis and Judith Schuler*

When my nephew, Scott, was a baby, his mom discovered by accident that the sound of the vacuum was the one thing that would consistently get him to sleep. You might have made a similar discovery while you were using the vacuum, dishwasher, or washing machine.

Some parents try to create absolute silence when they put their babies down to sleep, which is unnecessary. Although a sudden, loud noise may startle, white noise has a calming effect. Monotonous noise reminds them of the sounds they heard in utero.

Your baby's slowly adjusting to the new world he has been born into, and any reminder of the womb—the only world he knew for nine months—will be soothing.

Affirmation: I'll calm my baby with white noise.

LOVEMAKING

*Six weeks after Ben's birth my obstetrician
declared me ready to resume sexual relations.
Whatever that meant.*

—Roberta Israeloff

When you get the okay from your doctor, the
idea of having sex may be exciting, dreadful, or
anything in between.

For many new moms, resuming lovemaking is
a relatively smooth process and a much-needed
source of pleasure and nourishment.

But if you're not ready—because you're
exhausted or uncomfortable, or because frankly,
it's the farthest thing from your mind—just be
honest. Ask your partner to be patient, and find
other ways to show your affection and be
intimate. Give yourself as much time as you
need for desire to return, as it surely will.

**Affirmation: Sooner or later, making love will
seem like a lovely idea.**

NURSING

A babe at the breast is as much pleasure as the bearing is pain.

—*Marion Zimmer Bradley*

If you're breast-feeding your baby, you probably made the decision while you were pregnant. Now that the baby is here and you've experienced nursing, you may want to reevaluate your decision.

Some women describe the pleasures of nursing as "exquisitely intimate" and "sensual and soothing." Nursing can also be difficult and challenging. It's repetitive, at times painful. You're never really sure whether the baby is getting enough. You're absolutely tied down to the baby's schedule. You may or may not be comfortable nursing in public.

If nursing is going smoothly, great. If you're struggling, give it some time and be patient with yourself. But always know that nursing isn't the only option.

Ultimately, your health and well-being are more important than whether you formula-feed or nurse. The pleasures are different, but your baby will be nourished either way.

Affirmation: I'm a good mother whether I nurse or formula-feed.

EQUAL PARENTING

"Equal parenting" does not work—the maternal fine-tuning never turns off.

—*Phyllis Schlafly*

While I agree that mothers have an almost innate ability to care for their children, I beg to differ with the conclusion that equal parenting is a doomed proposition.

Mothers are not inherently more capable or necessary than fathers. For equal parenting to exist, mothers don't need to turn off their "fine-tuning." Many modern fathers are every bit as tuned in to parenting as their female counterparts.

Fathers have made important strides in becoming as involved in their children's lives as mothers. More and more fathers care for their children (rather than "baby-sit" them occasionally).

Given their cultural conditioning, men and women may parent differently. But mothers and fathers should be viewed equally capable and be equally appreciated. With equal parenting, everyone benefits: Fathers and mothers support each other, and babies get two capable, confident parents.

Affirmation: Equal parenting works.

CONTRACEPTION

Let me join in the chorus of people who should be telling you, YOU CAN GET PREGNANT WHILE YOU ARE NURSING, AND YOU CAN GET PREGNANT EVEN IF YOU HAVEN'T HAD A PERIOD YET.

—*Vicki Iovine*

Many people believe that nursing women can't conceive. They claim it's an evolutionary safeguard, ensuring that women space the births of their children, thus increasing the species' chance for survival.

Well, forget it. It's simply not true. The fact that most nursing mothers don't get pregnant has less to do with evolution than it does with the leaky breasts, cracked nipples, dry vagina, and extreme exhaustion that accompany lactation.

But nursing mothers resume lovemaking sooner or later, despite physical obstacles. And nursing mothers can in fact get pregnant, whether their periods have made an appearance or not.

If you aren't crazy about the idea of getting pregnant again, it's best to take precautions.

Affirmation: Nursing mothers can get pregnant.

LOVE

After the baby was born, I remember thinking that no one had ever told me how much I would love my child.

—Nora Ephron

People probably tried to tell you, but it just didn't register. You listened politely as your best friend bubbled with her intense love for her baby. You heard other women go on and on extolling the joys of motherhood, and you wondered if they were exaggerating just a little bit.

They weren't. Until you have a baby, you simply can't understand and appreciate the depth of passion and protectiveness a mother feels toward her child. It's unlike the love you experience in any other relationship. It floods you with tenderness, overwhelms you with gratitude.

Affirmation: Now I know how much I love my baby.

IMPROVISATION

*New parents quickly learn that raising children is
a kind of desperate improvisation.*

—Bill Cosby

The saying "Fake it till you make it" applies
beautifully to parenthood.

Especially in the beginning, you make up for
your inexperience by constantly improvising. You
try one thing, then another, mixing hearsay with
instinct, combining your mother's advice with the
latest parenting books, and experimenting until
you get it right.

One new mother described herself as a
"research scientist" trying out every formula in
an effort to find one her baby wasn't allergic to.
Another mother, in a desperate attempt to get
some rest, learned to attach a string to her baby's
cradle, which she pulled to rock it when her baby
cried during the night.

If there were only two words of advice for new
parents, they might be: *Whatever works.*

Affirmation: I'll learn to improvise.

COMMITMENT

[S]ome of us stammered through, "Will you m-m-ma-rrrry m-m-me?" and then hemmed and hawed about having a baby.... Why? For the same reason we stop at the video return pile— even though we've got exactly the video we want for the night, what if there's something better?
—James Douglas Barron

Some men fear commitment when it comes to marriage or a long-term relationship, and they're downright terrified of it when it comes to fatherhood. They're afraid to completely give themselves to family life because they wonder if "something better" is just around the bend.

If fear of commitment is keeping your partner from being an equal parent, know that he must work out this issue on his own. All you can do is love him, support him, and show him that creating a family can be the best experience in life.

With time, he'll come to realize that there may not be "something better" out there, and even if there were, he wouldn't trade his life for it.

Affirmation: My partner will commit to father-hood in his own way and his own time.

GIVING

*While you can quarrel with a grownup, how
can you quarrel with a newborn baby who
has stretched out his little arms for you to pick
him up?*

—Maria von Trapp

You get up in the middle of the night to feed,
diaper, and put the baby back to bed for the
eighth time. When you're met with an instant
encore of wails, it's tough to feel anything but
despair. But all you can do is throw up your hands
and laugh. Or cry.

These early days are a time of nonstop giving.
And giving. And more giving. There are few
tangible rewards. At times you feel resentful, and
rightfully so. You feel like screaming, "Shut up
and go to sleep!" but instead you reach down
and pick up the baby again.

Eventually you're rewarded. One blissful
morning you'll awake to sunshine and suddenly
realize your baby has slept through the night, and
you'll know you helped your baby reach an
important milestone.

Affirmation: Life will get easier.

DEPRESSION

Noble deeds and hot baths are the best cures for depression.

—Dodie Smith

Postpartum blues, exhaustion, boredom, anxiety, and profound feelings of isolation are all normal responses in the early months of motherhood.

If you're experiencing some of these feelings some of the time, there's no cause for concern. If, however, you're experiencing most of these feelings most of the time, you may need professional care. You may have postpartum depression, which is more than a case of the blues.

Assuming you're in the "sometimes" category, then do heed Dodie Smith's advice. Noble deeds and hot baths are terrific antidotes. Most likely, you've done many noble deeds; constant sacrifice is the norm for new moms.

Hot baths, on the other hand, require you to set aside time. Make a commitment to nurture yourself on a daily basis with hot baths, nourishing food, loving friends, and as much rest and relaxation as you can manage.

Affirmation: There are ways to lift my spirits.

CHILD CARE

*There is not even a name for what I am
searching for. Nanny? Too starch and British.
Sitter? Too transient to describe someone who
(please God) shows up every morning. Mother?
Bite your tongue!*

—Anna Quindlen

Whether you're searching for someone to watch
your child forty hours a week or a few hours on a
Saturday night, there really isn't an adequate job
title for the position. What word could possibly
describe what you're looking for?

You want a warm and nurturing individual
who'll love your child as much as you do, a clone
of yourself with the wisdom of Solomon and the
experience of Dr. Spock. You want someone
dependable and responsible, who'll never let you
down or leave you in the lurch.

It's a lot to ask. But it's not too much to ask for
the sake of your child's well-being and your own
peace of mind, because there's no greater security
than knowing your child is in good hands.

**Affirmation: I'll look until I find the right person
to care for my baby.**

MONITORS

*Sometimes your baby monitor may pick up other
people's monitors. Also remember that other
people's monitors may pick up yours.*
                                        —Jeanne Murphy

A baby monitor is a wonderful device. But it's
a little unsettling when you hear crying in the
monitor, only to rush into the nursery to find it's
interference from another monitor. Some monitors
have also been known to pick up conversations
from cell phones, cordless phones, and police
scanners, which no doubt startles mothers.

Worst yet, your monitor may transmit your
conversations to someone else's ears. Inevitably,
this only happens when you're telling your baby
about your hemorrhoids, when you're warbling a
2:00 A.M. lullaby, or when you're gossiping about
the neighborhood kids.

Your best bet is to pay a little extra for a
monitor that operates on a frequency designed
to block out most interference. Otherwise, be
prepared to hear all and be heard by all.

Affirmation: I'll be careful with baby monitors.

FORGETFULNESS

"I think all my brain cells came out with the after birth!"

—Beth Wilson Saavedra

An elephant never forgets, but you're no elephant. You're a new mother.

Since your baby's arrival, you've probably discovered that more and more things have slipped your memory. You rush to the grocery store, only to forget what you needed to buy. You forget to return phone calls. You can't find your keys. You make a detailed to-do list to boost your memory, and within five minutes of finishing it, you forget where you put it.

Consider your memory loss a blessing, not a curse. It's your maternal instinct's way to make sure you focus all your attention on the baby.

Affirmation: I'll remember that new mothers are forgetful.

INFLUENCE

God lends you your children until they're about eighteen years old. If you haven't made your points with them by then, it's too late.

—*Betty Ford*

Actually, your child is always on loan, whether she's eight weeks, eight months, or eighteen. She belongs to herself, on temporary loan for a brief period of time to be cuddled, counseled, loved, and cared for to the best of your ability.

As the poet Kahlil Gibran said, "They come through you but not from you, / And though they are with you yet they belong not to you."

By being a good parent, you'll prepare your child to be her own keeper.

Affirmation: I have guardianship, not ownership, of my child.

PETS

*The cat who purrs so sweetly cannot fathom why
her place in our bed has been taken by this one
who cries.*

—Susan Eisenberg

Adjusting to a new baby is difficult for your entire
family, including your pet. Your cat or dog used to
be the center of attention and ruler of the house,
but the baby has usurped that position.

There are two things to keep in mind when
you have a baby and a pet. One, your baby needs
to be safe at all times. Never leave your baby
unsupervised around your pet. Watch your pet
closely for signs of aggression. If this is the case,
don't let the pet near the baby at any time.

Two, your pet still needs your love. Make
feeding and playing with your pet part of your
daily routine. Make sure your pet knows that even
if life has changed with a baby in the house, it
doesn't mean you can't love each "member" of
the family.

**Affirmation: My pet needs to adjust to life with
a baby, too.**

THERMOMETERS

*Prepare the thermometer and bare baby's bottom,
speaking reassuringly as you do.*
—*Arlene Eisenberg, Heidi E. Murkoff,
and Sandee E. Hathaway*

Who are the reassuring words for—the baby
or you?

The first time you take your baby's temperature
with a rectal thermometer, you may find yourself
more than a little nervous. No matter if you use
Vaseline and comforting words, you worry that
the experience will be excruciating for your baby.

There are other ways to take your baby's temperature, such as with an axillary thermometer
under the armpit. Ear thermometers are relatively
new and are fast, anxiety-free alternatives to
rectal thermometers.

However you take your baby's temp, try to do
it calmly and carefully. Your child's health is at
stake, and a few moments of discomfort (for all
those involved) are certainly worthwhile.

**Affirmation: I'll carefully take my baby's
temperature.**

A DAY IN THE LIFE

Before you had the baby, you sped, rarely used your blinker, and talked nonstop on your cell phone. The first few trips with the baby made you shape up, but now that you're used to the little passenger in the back seat, you find yourself reviving your old habits. That's okay, right?

Having a baby in the car shouldn't stop you from driving the legal speed limit, but it should keep you from taking dangerous risks behind the wheel. You shouldn't take such risks even if you're driving solo.

Being a mother gives you a new perspective on life. You should, of course, keep your baby safe, but you should also take good care of yourself. Driving carelessly may have been no big deal before you became a mother, but now you have a responsibility to always be there for your baby.

So drive the speed limit, use your blinkers, and turn off the phone. Not doing so can cause accidents, and accidents can mean irreparable harm or even death to you and your baby.

Affirmation: Being a good driver keeps me and my baby safe.

NAPTIME

When you hear people say, "All they do is sleep," don't believe it.

—Laura Zahn

In my Expecting Change workshops, expectant mothers play the Baby Reality Game. Participants roll the dice to determine how many naps their babies will take. If, how long, and how often a newborn naps separates the rested from the ragged, the patient from the irritable, the relatively sane from those on the verge of a nervous breakdown.

In reality, it's even odds whether a baby will nap. And if he does, you can never know how long a nap will last. Anticipating a solid two-hour nap, you plan to tackle housework—then the baby wakes up in fifteen minutes. Or you predict only a half-hour, so you don't bother to lie down yourself—then he sleeps three and a half hours.

Since naps are highly unpredictable, it's best do whatever is highest priority. For most new moms it's sleep.

Affirmation: I'll prioritize my time when the baby naps.

TENDERNESS

*I stumble into the nursery, pick up my son…and
as he fastens himself to me like a tiny sucking
minnow, I am flooded with tenderness.*
—Sara Davidson

No matter how tired you are, no matter how
many times you've stumbled in the darkness to
heed your baby's tireless cry to be fed, there's
something profoundly moving in that instant
when your bodies reconnect or when she snug-
gles in close to take the bottle. Your newborn's
delicacy, dependency, and trust overwhelms you
with tenderness.

This isn't to say that you always feel happy or
even willing to nurse or bottle-feed. There are
times when you're too worn out, too depleted to
care. But even then you find the strength to offer
sustenance and are deeply satisfied by your ability
to nourish your child.

Affirmation: My child fills me with tenderness.

DAY CARE

There is no contradiction between being a good mother and leaving a child in the care of another adult for part of each day.
        —Sirgay Sanger and John Kelly

Some mothers find it hard to really believe there's no conflict between being a good mother and leaving their children in day care. Their frightened inner voices say, "If I'm not with my child, will he be okay?" Their judgmental inner voices say, "Good mothers don't pawn their children off on strangers."

I believe mothers must silence these voices. They're false and destructive.

But *you* must decide what's best for you and your child. That may mean opting for day care, staying at home, or arranging a schedule to do both. Whatever you decide, it'll be the right decision for you, and your inner voice will say, "I'm a good mother. My child is fine. I'm caring for my child the best way I can."

Affirmation: Regardless of whether I send my child to day care, I'm a good mother.

INTIMACY

Our life was one long conversation about how tiring our days were.

—Roberta Israeloff

This sentiment expresses the frustration so many couples feel while trying to connect in the wake of sleepless nights and demanding days with an infant.

Is it inevitable for your relationship to be reduced to such frustration?

Yes and no. On one hand, it's realistic during these first weeks and months to feel overwhelmed and frustrated. Caring for your baby is a huge adjustment for you both; it's natural to miss the undivided attention and devotion you used to share.

On the other hand, there are ways, even in the midst of all this, to enhance intimacy: listen without criticism, support each other, thank each other for the contributions you make to your newly enlarged family, share your hopes and fears along with the details of your day—however tiring they were. All this helps you stay connected and close.

Affirmation: Let's stay close.

OVERSCHEDULING

*Every day, make a commitment to do only
one activity.*

—*Veteran mom*

This advice comes from a woman who had just
had her third child. "With my first two kids, I tried
to pack a million things into each day," she recalls.
"I'd care for them while cleaning the refrigerator,
running errands, and catching up with a friend on
the phone. And every day I ended up frustrated
and exhausted. So now I only do one thing, and
anything else that gets accomplished is a bonus."

This is advice well taken, especially in the first
few months following childbirth. There's no point
in running yourself ragged. Make a list of everything that needs to be done, prioritize it, and then
do only what's first on the list. If anything else
gets finished, great. If not, you're doing enough
as it is.

Affirmation: I won't stretch myself too thin.

A DAY IN THE LIFE

*The mail arrives—an invitation to a party given
by your closest friend. You call to RSVP, adding,
"Of course, we'll have to bring the baby." There's
a pause, then she replies, "Well, actually, we
were only planning on adults." You're not ready
to leave the baby with a sitter, and you're a little
upset. What do you do?*

First ask politely whether your baby can be an
exception—since she's so young. After all, this
is your best friend; it can't hurt to ask.

If the answer is still no, then you have a few
other options. You can try a baby sitter, since
you'll need to make that leap at some point.
Or you and your partner can take turns, each
attending the party for a short time while the
other stays home with the baby. If all else fails,
you can politely decline the invitation.

The only option you *don't* have is to bring the
baby anyway or to turn this into a full-scale war
with your friend. Next time, consider having the
party at your house so you don't have to go
through this again.

Affirmation: I'm willing to compromise.

FEEDING

Feeding time provides more than good nutrition for your newborn. It is an opportunity to hold, cuddle, and make eye contact.... It is a special time during which you can talk to Baby and tell [him] how special [he] is.

—Becky Daniel

When you nurse or bottle-feed, your baby is quiet, focused, snuggled within your arms. What a wonderful time to connect as mother and child.

Don't just zone out or turn on the TV. Every time you feed your baby, you have an opportunity to bond with your baby. You're bound to each other, and for that short time, you can love each other freely and without distraction.

Nourish your baby with sweet kisses as well as sweet milk or formula. Nourish him with gentle caresses, adoring smiles, and loving words. You have the power to help your baby grow strong of body, mind, and soul.

Affirmation: At feeding time, I'll physically and emotionally nourish my baby.

A DAY IN THE LIFE

It's a drag to get out of bed every time the baby cries in the middle of the night. You've been reading a lot about family beds, but opinions vary. You wish someone would come out with a final say about it.

There really isn't a final say on the subject of family beds—just a lot of pros and cons.

Pros: Having the baby in your bed makes it easier to attend to her nighttime needs; some babies cry less when they're in a family bed. Sharing a bed is a cozy way to bond as a family. In fact, it's the norm in many cultures.

Cons: Your baby's a noisy sleeper. It may be difficult when you want to be a "couple" rather than a "family." And no disrespect to other cultures, but in this culture, most children sleep in their own beds. If you keep a family bed now, it may be harder for her to adjust to her own bed down the road. Plus, many experts say there's a risk of smothering a baby in an adult bed.

There's a lot to consider, but the final say about a family bed is up to you.

Affirmation: I'll weigh the pros and cons of a family bed.

ADVICE

As time passes we all get better at blazing a trail through the thicket of advice.

—Margot Bennett

And there's a lot of advice out there! Parenting web sites spout tried and true tips. Experienced, well-meaning friends and relatives lend insight. Even your coworkers and neighbors may offer words of wisdom—with or without your asking.

Some advice is helpful. Some is irrelevant. And some just makes you feel defensive or pressured.

Here's one more piece of unsolicited advice: Listen carefully to outside opinions, then trust your gut. Ninety-nine percent of the time, you're the expert. Ultimately, your everyday, hands-on experience gives you the wisdom and knowledge you need.

There's a ton of information, yet no clear-cut manual for mothering. Whether you're deciding when to introduce rice cereal or choosing child care, consider your child's needs and preferences, make the most informed decision possible, and don't let other people's opinions sway your confidence.

Affirmation: The best advice is to trust my own opinion.

NURSING

I tried all the conventional ruses (pumping my breasts, drinking beer, eating potatoes) but my milk supply gradually and remorselessly dried up. I felt that I had failed.

—Sylvia Ann Hewlett

This confession by scholar and author Sylvia Ann Hewlett makes me sad. How many other new mothers have felt exactly the same sense of failure when, despite their best efforts, nursing simply didn't work out?

If you've given everything you've got to breast-feeding, but for some reason it isn't turning out to be right for you or your baby, then give it up without feeling guilty.

If anything, give yourself credit. Count every single day of nursing as a great gift you've given your baby. And know that you have been nothing less than a great success to your baby.

Affirmation: I'm doing my best to nurse my baby.

TIME

We just call each other on the phone and whine about how we don't have time to get together.
—Cathy Guisewite

When my friend Jan had a baby, she was desperate to find a part-time sitter. "Just put up a notice at schools or the grocery store," I kept encouraging her. It took her almost three months to follow my advice. Why? She had a baby. She didn't have time to look for a sitter. If she had had enough time to run around town posting notices, she probably wouldn't have needed a sitter in the first place!

You see the dilemma. In these early weeks, even the littlest things that could make life easier—arranging child care, getting together with other moms and babies, even making a haircut appointment—take more time and energy than you can muster.

Make the time. Find the energy. It's well worth it to make those field trips into the outside world. They're small investments with huge returns.

Affirmation: I'm willing to make an investment of time.

PRESSURE

*In some ways you go through motherhood in an
under-siege mentality. You never admit how hard
things are till they're safely behind you.*
                                        —*Liz Rosenberg*

In my photo album are photos of me with my
brand-new baby. I look like a strung-out drug
addict. My glazed eyes have deep, dark circles
under them. I'm wearing a soiled T-shirt, clutching
a cup of coffee, standing knee-deep in what
appears to be a pile of dirty laundry and
unopened mail.

In retrospect, it's hard to imagine how anyone
survives the ordeals of early motherhood: sleep
deprivation, constant uncertainty, the horror
that something may happen to the baby, the loss
of control.

You'll look back on these first few weeks and
months and be amazed that you got through
them in one piece. But while they're happening,
you simply put one foot in front of the other,
meeting each challenge.

Affirmation: I'll make it through this.

CREATIVITY

Another thing that seems quite helpful to the creative process is having babies.
— Faye Weldon

Giving and nurturing life releases a wellspring of creativity. You want to express yourself by writing poetry, playing the piano, or taking that water-color class you've always wanted to try.

The problem is finding the time to be creative—making the commitment to release the artist within you without compromising the other demands in your life.

There's only one way to do it, and that's to *do* it. Let your creativity loose by setting aside fifteen minutes a day to draw in a sketchbook or scribble in your journal. Or plan one day a month to check out the latest art exhibit or to attend a concert where all you have to do is sit back, close your eyes, and let the music fill your creative soul.

Affirmation: I'll nurture the artist in myself.

TRIAL AND ERROR

If it isn't working, change it.

—*Vicky Stewart*

I heard Vicky say this at a friend's baby shower as each guest offered her best advice on parenthood. She went on to elaborate: "If your baby's crying and you're feeding him, stop. If you're not feeding him, start. If you're standing up, sit down; if you're sitting down, stand up."

As obvious as it seems, this is sound advice, especially during these first months when your baby can't tell you what's wrong, what he needs, or what would make it right.

Most of the time, parenting is guesswork, and trial and error often works best.

Affirmation: I'll learn what works by trial and error.

BABY SITTERS

When you're looking for a sitter for your baby, be warned: Everyone looks like a hired killer.
                                        —*Vicki Iovine*

It's terrifying to leave your precious newborn with a sitter for the first time. Even if the sitter is a close friend or a grandparent, horrible visions make it nearly impossible to enjoy yourself. What if the baby cries and cries and the sitter can't calm her? What if she loses her pacifier or gets put on her stomach instead of on her back? What if your cell phone needs charging, and there's no way to reach you? What if, God forbid, there's a fire, and you never see your child again?

You can "what if" yourself right back home if you don't trust that your baby will be well taken care of. No one loves or understands your child as well as you do, but you still have to take this first leap of faith and leave her in someone else's care.

Affirmation: Leaving my baby is hard, but I must take a leap of faith.

SUPERMOM

I know that somewhere there must be mothers who in one week go back to their regular clothes; who appear at their desks as if nothing happened, whistling.

—*Phyllis Chesler*

This Supermom myth creates pressure, guilt, and a feeling of inadequacy. So does the myth that somewhere there are mothers who in one week slip into little black dresses and throw lavish dinner parties, where they sip wine, pass around photos of their lovely babies, and catch up on the latest gossip.

Forget it. Those women don't exist. Or if they do, they have full-time live-in nannies. Most women are just like you: haggard, exhausted, overwhelmed, and determined to make motherhood work.

Don't make it harder by trying to live up to impossible ideals.

Affirmation: I won't believe the Supermom myths.

BEGINNINGS

You know the beginning is the most important part of any work.

—*Plato*

What a beginning this is—you made the commitment to be a parent. But once your child is born, his life is somewhat out of your hands. He enters the world a distinct individual whom you can shape but cannot mold to your liking.

Before I had children, I was a great advocate of nurture over nature. Once my children were born, I learned otherwise. Each was different: Zoe was an "old soul"—sensitive, wise, and introspective even as an infant. Evan was as new as the morning's sunrise—fresh, wondrous, and filled with innocence and joy.

You begin the work. Then it becomes your lifelong job to love your child enough to let him be who he is, not who you want him to be.

Affirmation: I've given my child a great start. Now I'll look forward to discovering who he is.

HOLIDAYS

Holidays
Have no pity.

—Eugenio Montale

The stretch between Thanksgiving and New Year's Day may be especially stressful for you. On top of your usually hectic schedule, you'll have relatives to visit, parties to attend, decorations to put up, meals to prepare, and gifts to buy—none of which is easy to do with a baby in tow.

But this will be your baby's first holiday experience, and you'll no doubt want it to be magical. If you can't see past the stressful, negative aspects of holiday preparation, your baby won't either.

So simplify the decorations and meals, and cut back on gifts. Do whatever it takes to renew your commitment to spirituality, family, friendship, and goodwill during this season. You can't teach your baby about the magic of the holiday season unless you believe in it, too.

Affirmation: I'll make the holidays magical for my baby and me.

SECURITY

Legal stuff: "An ounce of prevention."
—Laura Zahn

When she was four, Zoe once asked, "If something happened to you and Daddy, where would we go?" Swallowing hard, I said, "You'd go live with Auntie Faith." There was a long pause before Evan, then two, asked, "How would we get there?" I was ready to explain wills, guardianship, and any number of other legal details, but all that concerned him was who would drive them to my sister Faith's house.

Right now, your baby is too young to ask such questions, but it's imperative that you ask yourself, "How would I manage if my partner died? How would he manage if I died? How would the baby manage if we both died?"

Contact a lawyer about wills and a financial planner about life insurance as soon as possible. Your family's security depends on it.

Affirmation: I'll plan for my family's security in case the unthinkable happens.

A DAY IN THE LIFE

Your baby sucks on everything—a pacifier, her thumb, her fingers, even her entire fist. Today you found her sucking her toes! You're a little worried that this is going too far. Shouldn't you discourage such behavior?

Babies have an intense need to suck. It's natural, and it provides comfort. Some babies like pacifiers and some enjoy sucking their fingers. Some babies even suck their thumbs in utero. Once babies are coordinated enough to grab their feet, the "five little piggies" often end up in their mouths, too.

So why discourage sucking? Your baby's hands and toes are sanitary. Sucking rarely leads to developmental problems down the road, and most children grow out of it easily by the time they're preschoolers.

Think of it this way: Can you suck your own toes? Probably not, unless you're a contortionist or unless you're willing to pop something out of joint. Let your baby enjoy this fringe benefit of being a baby.

Affirmation: I understand that my baby needs to suck something—even toes!

THOUGHTS

What is the little one thinking about?
Very wonderful things, no doubt!
Unwritten history!
Unfathomed mystery!

—J. G. Holland

So what *is* your baby thinking about? It's a lovely question to ponder.

Is he thinking about the hunger pangs in his stomach, anticipating his next feeding? Is he thinking about the noise the rattle makes or what those words mean when people talk to him? Is he thinking about how he came to be, how he happened upon this house and these particular people?

You can ponder, wonder, and guess all you want, but your baby's thoughts are fathomless mysteries. The only thing you can hope is that your baby is thinking about how much you love him.

Affirmation: Baby, what are you thinking?

GROWTH

Babies don't need vacations, but I still see them at the beach.

—Steven Wright

Does it ever occur to you that babies have it better than anyone else? All they have to do is eat and sleep and be rocked and be cuddled, right? You look at them, look at yourself, and wish you could trade places, even for an hour or two.

But appearances are deceiving. Your child is doing a great deal; she's growing; developing a personality; learning language; and figuring out the mechanics of crawling, walking, and drinking from a cup.

Being a baby may look like nothing when it's compared to running a household or making a living. But your baby's life is every bit as exhausting and challenging as yours—just in a different way.

Affirmation: My baby's life is challenging.

"WORKING MOTHERS"

The phrase "working mother" is redundant.
—Jane Sellman

Every time I hear the words *working mother*, I have to keep myself from throwing a fit. The term makes me mad because it implies a distinction between mothers who work inside the home and those who work outside the home. It implies, not too subtly, that stay-at-home mothers do not really work, certainly not at a bona fide career.

In fact, all mothers work. The demands of being home all day are no less important than the demands of juggling a child and an outside career. They're just different. Both deserve respect, and both deserve support.

It's time to eliminate the term *working mother*. The next time you hear someone use it, turn to him or her and say, "Excuse me, but what do you mean?"

Affirmation: All mothers work.

PEACE

*I remember moments of peace when for
some reason it was possible to go to the
bathroom alone.*

—*Adrienne Rich*

Did you ever imagine you'd celebrate going to the
bathroom alone?

The simple moments of peace you once took
for granted assume greater value when there's a
baby clamoring for your attention. Sleeping past
eight o'clock, reading the newspaper, going
grocery shopping alone—now these are
extraordinary luxuries, the tantalizing subjects
of daydreams.

When you have a baby, you relinquish your
most basic freedoms, then gradually regain them.
It makes you fiercely protective and far more
appreciative when you do find a rare moment
of peace.

**Affirmation: I will make the most of my moments
of peace.**

BARGAINS

Little Tykes toys sell out at garage sales by 8:00 A.M. Shop early!

—*Jeanne Murphy*

If you have a baby and limited disposable income, you'll probably find yourself scouting out bargains at garage sales, swap meets, and secondhand stores.

Babies need lots of equipment and lots of clothes, which cost lots of money. The worse part about it is that babies grow out of these things faster than parents can say, "Bankruptcy!"

Some things you need to buy new, such as car seats, to ensure that they meet current safety standards. Other items will work just fine if they've been slightly used by another family. Swap meets and garage sales save you tons of money and are great ways to meet other parents.

Just remember: You're not the only mom who's scouring sales for great deals—get there early!

Affirmation: Shopping at swap meets and garage sales saves money.

ALTRUISM

When thou art feeble, old and gray,
My healthy arm shall be thy stay,
And I will soothe thy pains away,
    My mother.

—*Jane Taylor*

When you resent caring for your baby day and night, you may be cheered to imagine that your child will someday care for you in your old age.

Although this is a touching thought, you shouldn't expect it. Right or wrong, we live in a culture where most families leave the elderly in the care of strangers. No matter how much he may love you, you simply can't assume he'll be able to tend to you day and night when you're older.

It's much better to set fantasies aside and instead reaffirm your motivation for your sacrifices. You don't care for your child just to get something in return. You care for him because above all else, you love him and want to give him more than he can ever give in return.

Affirmation: Loving my baby is its own reward.

BATH TIME

No flower is as fragrant as a baby after a bath.
—Sherri Waas Shunfenthal

Babies do smell wonderful after a bath. The pure, sweet scent of a clean baby is intoxicating—which makes all the effort you put into bath time worthwhile.

Some babies don't like baths. They hate to be naked, they don't like to get wet, and they can't stay still long enough to get properly cleaned. If your baby doesn't like baths, you probably spend most of your time soothing and distracting her while you try to wash her body and face in one quick swoop.

Even if your baby likes baths, bath time can still be quite a production. You feel as if you need more than two hands to hold a wet, slippery baby and all the towels, washcloths, cotton balls, soaps, sponges, and rubber duckies.

However bath time plays itself out, it's a comfort to know that the result will be a sweet, soft, fragrant baby.

Affirmation: The smell of my clean baby is a great reward after bath time.

CONVERSATION

Even if your husband is nearly as obsessed with your baby as you are, our advice is to try to avoid starting every conversation with him by saying, "You'll never believe what the baby did today!"
—Vicki Iovine

Sure, you'd love to start a conversation with your partner that doesn't involve the baby, but...well... what else is there to talk about? Try these conversation starters:

- "Let's order a pizza and rent a movie tonight. Any suggestions?"
- "My sister called. Boy, is she having a crisis."
- "I've been thinking. Is it time to get a bigger TV?"
- "I went to Victoria's Secret today. Want to see what I bought?"

See? You can have a conversation without the words *baby*, *poop*, *cry*, or *spit-up*. You may have to be a little creative, but keeping in touch with your partner and life outside the baby is worth it.

Affirmation: I can start a conversation that isn't about the baby.

CRYING

This is the Basic Baby Mood Cycle:
Mood One: Just about to cry.
Mood Two: Crying.
Mood Three: Just finished crying.

—Dave Barry

There's nothing especially amusing about those days when it seems all your baby does is cry, cry some more, and cry until he falls asleep from exhaustion, only to wake up crying again.

You try feeding, rocking, walking in circles till you're ready to collapse, and the baby still won't stop crying.

At these moments, it's natural to feel incompetent, to think, "If I were a good mother, I'd know what to do." You feel helpless, frustrated, and ready to burst into tears yourself.

The crying will stop, but sometimes you can simply do nothing but wait. Sometimes babies cry and cry for no apparent reason. Try not to take on the blame.

Affirmation: Sometimes there's nothing I can do when my baby cries.

A DAY IN THE LIFE

Your say you want your partner to be an equal parent, but every time he tries, you take the baby out of his arms. You criticize how he burps her, you make fun of how he diapers her. He's starting to feel as if he can't do anything right.

Of course he is! How else could he feel when all his efforts are criticized and dismissed?

Your partner's desire to be an equal parent is admirable. However, this situation requires compromise from both of you if it's going to work. It's natural for some moms, especially stay-at-home moms, to have trouble letting others tend their babies, but you need to let go a little and allow your partner to parent. And your partner needs to be open to your feedback, as long as your suggestions are respectful and in the baby's best interest.

The important thing to remember is that parenting is much easier when you support, not criticize, each other.

Affirmation: I'll share the responsibility of parenting.

SHARING

The joys of parents are secret, and so are their griefs and fears.

—Francis Bacon

So often you keep your parenting triumphs and troubles to yourself. You censor your pride for your child's accomplishments for fear you'll sound as if you're bragging. Likewise, you remain silent about what's difficult or trying because you're afraid and ashamed of what other people might think.

In truth, all parents are proud of their children's accomplishments and uneasy about their struggles. So it makes much more sense for parents to support one another than to isolate themselves. Together, you can celebrate when your children shine, cope when they struggle, share ideas and encouragement, and, most importantly, simply lend sympathetic ears.

Affirmation: I needn't isolate myself from other parents.

SLEEP

There was never child so lovely but his mother was glad to get him asleep.

—*Ralph Waldo Emerson*

Aah! Your child is never more lovely than when he's nestled peacefully under his covers.

Many new mothers, exhausted from a day of constantly attending to the endless needs of their newborns, stand adoringly over the cribs, admiring their sweet babies in slumber. Those heavy lids; warm, flushed cheeks; and damp, curled fingers wrapped around a teddy bear are a welcome sight.

Tonight, take a moment to peek into your baby's bed before crawling into your own.

Affirmation: My sleeping baby is precious.

ORDER

*When you have a child, things are
unscheduled chaos.*

—Wendy Shulman

Forget planning. Relinquish your fantasy of the
three-hour nap your baby will take at exactly
2:00 P.M. Throw away the list of everything you
need to do today—grocery shopping, checking in
at the office, writing thank-you notes for baby
gifts—because it probably won't happen.

You were used to a certain amount of order.
You operated on a timetable, had things organized, made appointments and kept them. Then
the baby arrived with the force of a cyclone
destroying everything in its path.

Don't spend precious energy being angry over
a timetable that's out of your hands. Relax your
expectations, batten down the hatches, settle in
until the storm passes. It's exciting. Unpredictable.
Rarely boring, especially if you can give yourself
over to the chaos—and peace—that befalls you.

**Affirmation: I'll let go of my need for
perfect order.**

IDENTITY

Every day there is less of me and more of the baby.
—Carol Itter

Early on, it's natural to feel as if your entire identity has been subsumed in motherhood. You spend every waking hour caring for your newborn. Her schedule predominates, her needs prevail, and her paraphernalia takes over the house. In the midst of it all, you feel as if you've lost any and all sense of self.

It's easy to lose yourself unless you make a special effort to do something at least once a day that reminds you of who you are. (Going to work doesn't count.) Get a sitter if you have to, then talk to a friend on the phone, read a magazine article that interests you, play tennis, go to a movie, or take a walk. Do anything that helps you recover your sense of self.

Affirmation: I won't lose my identity.

OVERSCHEDULING

When your schedule leaves you brain dead and stressed to exhaustion, it's time to…say no. Be brutal.

—Marilyn Ruman

Motherhood adds an extra layer of stress to your already overscheduled life. Whether you're home full-time or balancing career and parenting, the pressures mount; it's impossible to add one more item to your to-do list without losing it.

Yet you find it so hard to say no when your church needs someone to bake cookies for the fundraiser or your neighbor needs a ride to work while her car is in the shop. You're afraid of disappointing other people. After all, what's one more errand, one more favor, when you're already going full tilt?

You need to say no. Saying no is a way of saying yes: yes to protecting your limited time and energy; yes to your health and well-being; yes to your sanity so you can concentrate on what truly matters the most.

Affirmation: I'll say yes to myself.

A DAY IN THE LIFE

You're ready to get your love life back on track, but how? Whenever you and your partner are in the mood, the baby needs to be fed, the laundry needs to be folded, supper needs to be cooked. Is your love life lost forever?

Being parents means you no longer have the luxury of doing whatever you want whenever you want. This includes eating when you're hungry, showering when you need to freshen up, and making love when you're in the mood.

Flexibility is the best remedy. Just as you must learn to eat and shower whenever the baby naps or is content in the swing, you must learn to make love when the opportunity—not the desire—arises.

At first, it may seem frustrating and awkward. But if you keep a sense of humor and spontaneity, you'll find these impromptu sessions exciting, fulfilling, and romantic—even if the baby cries right when things get good.

Affirmation: We'll make love whenever we have an opportunity.

CAREER

I did not fear being able to work again so much as never wanting to work again.

—Jane Lazarre

If your maternity leave is almost over and you're planning to return to your job, you may be in a mild state of panic. You may worry that your ambition has permanently vanished, that your mind has turned to mush, that you couldn't possibly concentrate—much less care—about anything other than your baby.

Never fear. Most mothers say that their drive and focus return naturally as they ease back into their jobs. If you're back on the job before your baby is three months old, give yourself a gold star simply for showing up. If you get to work (more or less) on time and have matching shoes and a slight semblance of order on your desk, you deserve a medal.

Balancing a family and a career requires organization, brains, and the ability to occasionally be two places at once, especially in the beginning. Little by little, you'll come to enjoy the complementary pleasures of motherhood and career.

Affirmation: Balancing a career and a family won't be a hard as I imagine.

BABY TALK

*My wife and I often summoned the grandparents
of our first baby and cried, "Look, poopoo!"*
—Bill Cosby

Babies are just so cute! Everything about them is
cute—even their bowel movements, rashes, and
spit-ups, which parents talk about enthusiastically
at the drop of a hat.

The truth is, no one but parents care. And
no one but parents find those sorts of things
cute. Even the most doting grandparents could
do without endless up-to-the-minute reports.

The need to convey such detailed information
is a passing stage, best shared with other
new parents.

Affirmation: I'll keep the details to a minimum.

CONFORMITY

Infancy conforms to nobody; all conform to it.
—Ralph Waldo Emerson

By this time, you've probably noticed that your life has conformed to your child's. You jump when he cries, you organize your schedule around his, you sleep when he sleeps, you venture out into the world only after making elaborate arrangements for his care.

This is how life is when you parent a baby. You conform to your child's style and pace, and sometimes you resent it. You yearn for the past, when you had the luxury of coming and going as you pleased, eating when you felt like it, following your own desires and goals without always accommodating another person—an uncompromising one at that.

The good news is, the older your child gets, the less you must conform. With age, he'll be more patient, more flexible, and less tyrannical. And when he reaches that age, you'll really appreciate it.

Affirmation: This conformity won't last forever.

OLDER CHILDREN

Just as you can have plenty of love for both your mom and dad, they can have plenty of love for both you and the baby.

—Fred Rogers

Easy for Mr. Rogers to say. But if you have an older child whose supremacy has been usurped by a brand-new baby, the older sibling may or may not be reassured by those words.

Here are some better words to try as your older child adjusts to the changes: "I know this is hard for you," and "For the next fifteen minutes, I'll play with you even if the baby has to wait," and "I love you even more than before."

Here are some words not to say: "You used to scream like that, too," and "I thought you wanted to be a big sister!"

Avoid dismissing the "big-kid blues." Instead, concentrate on anything that enables your older child to express her feelings, letting her know that she can be frustrated without losing your love.

Affirmation: I'll help my older child adjust to our new family.

SKILL BUILDING

Parenthood remains the greatest single preserve of the amateur.

—Alvin Toffler

What other full-time endeavor in the world has no job description, no formal training, no prerequisite other than desire?

Yet what more does anybody really need? All parents are amateurs in the beginning. By the time their children are out of diapers, all parents could lead training seminars.

For parenting, time and experience are the only teachers. You try your best, make mistakes, learn from them, and improve as you go.

It's the only way to become a professional parent.

Affirmation: I'm learning on the job.

SELF-CARE

*You give up, or postpone, many of the pleasures
you once enjoyed, such as eating when you are
hungry…going to sleep when you are tired.*
　　　　　　　　　　　　　　　—Lydia Davis

Sacrifice, sacrifice, sacrifice. It's the mantra of
motherhood. But you shouldn't sacrifice your
health and well-being. You need to know yourself,
know your limits, and make sure you're getting
the basics.

　　Some people only need five hours of sleep.
But if sleep is imperative for you, resist the urge
to watch late-night television and go to bed
immediately when the baby goes down. Some
people can live on two doughnuts for lunch. But
if a healthy diet is your priority, be sure there's
nutritious food in the refrigerator and make
time to eat regular meals.

　　Being a good mother means taking good care
of your baby. It also means taking good care of
your health.

Affirmation: I'll take care of my health.

LANGUAGE

Researchers say that children learn languages most easily between birth and age 10.
—Glade B. Curtis and Judith Schuler

One, two, three… *Uno, dos, tres…*

Your baby has an amazing capacity for language acquisition. Presumably, your baby's primary language will be English, but he's also capable of learning another language or even several other languages simultaneously.

If English isn't your native language, this can be a wonderful way to pass your mother tongue on to the newest generation of your family. Even if English is your native language, teaching your baby a different language is a great way to broaden his horizons.

Affirmation: I'll share another language with my child.

ESSENCE

In their sympathies, children feel nearer animals than adults.

—Jessamyn West

Like an animal, your baby has limited language—she cannot criticize, negotiate, or lie. Like an animal, she's often driven by a basic need for food, shelter, sleep—not by a need for material goods, power, or prestige. Like an animal, your baby offers unconditional love—not love based on expectations.

The animal world is natural, primitive, and pure. Soon enough, your baby will join the adult world with all its complexities and shortcomings. But for now, notice how your baby is like an animal and perhaps even learn from it.

Affirmation: In many ways, my baby is more like an animal than an adult.

A DAY IN THE LIFE

You just put your three-month-old in day care, and you're a wreck. Your best friend just took a leave of absence to stay home with her three-month-old, and she's a wreck, too. You can't stop calling your day-care provider, and she can't stop calling work. You both thought you were deeply committed to your respective decisions, but now you're not sure.

You and your friend have made different decisions, but you have the same problem: letting go. Choosing to put your child in day care or to put your career on hold is a drastic life change. Nevertheless, you must learn to let go so you can devote your full attention to the life you've chosen, not to the life you've set aside.

If either of you *can't* let go, then it may mean you're not comfortable with your decision. You may need to renegotiate maternity leave so you have more time to consider your options before you commit to any decision. You may want to join a new moms' support group to sort out your feelings, whatever they may be.

Affirmation: I'll do what's best for my baby and myself, which includes learning to let go.

ADMIRATION

*Parents of young children should realize that few
people, and maybe no one, will find their
children as enchanting as they do.*

—Barbara Walters

I still haven't quite figured this out, as evidenced
by the dog-eared photographs of my children I
insist on pulling out of my purse and shoving
under the noses of utter strangers at dinner
parties. Inevitably, I'm insulted when the photos
are met with cool glances and polite acknowl-
edgments instead of the oohs, aahs, and
"Shouldn't they model?" comments I expect.

All parents think their children are the most
gorgeous, the most brilliant, the most talented.
And no one else is as captivated by their children
as they are.

It's sad but true: You may get more rave reviews
on the new bathroom wallpaper than on your
baby's breathtaking face—except when grandparents arrive. Now, there's an appreciative audience!

**Affirmation: No one is more captivated by my
child than I am.**

GODLINESS

God couldn't be everywhere, so he invented mothers.

—*Jewish proverb*

This is a double-edged sword. On one hand, you're flattered by the idea that motherliness is next to godliness. On the other hand, you feel pressured to come up with the godlike energy, love, and resourcefulness required for the job.

It's great to have confidence in your ability to handle the rigors of motherhood—whether it's staying up all night nursing a sick baby or summoning your last shred of patience to retrieve the pacifier from under the swing for the fourteenth time.

However, you need to keep your expectations in check. Being a mother means being human. Omnipresent, yes. Divine, perhaps. But it's just fine if you make a mistake or need a break. After all, on the seventh day God rested.

Affirmation: I don't have to be godlike.

PREOCCUPATION

When you are a mother, you are never really alone in your thoughts.

—Sophia Loren

A corner of your consciousness is always occupied by thoughts of your child. When your infant finally—*finally*—goes down after an arduous 4:00 A.M. feeding, you sleep at attention, waiting for him to wake up. You develop eyes in the back of your head so you can cook supper and still spot your baby teetering on the brink of disaster.

Even when you're apart, you hold your child in your mind. In the middle of the library fundraiser, you suddenly make a note to tell your day-care provider that turnips are out of the question.

Your child is ever present in your thoughts. Even when you can't be with him, you carry him near your heart everywhere you go. Whether you're halfway across town at the grocery store or halfway across the country on a business trip, you worry and wonder if he's happy and safe.

Affirmation: My child is always in my thoughts.

VALUE

To nourish children and raise them against odds is in any time, any place, more valuable than to fix bolts in cars or design nuclear weapons.
—*Marilyn French*

Some women feel vaguely apologetic about motherhood. I wish this weren't so. Even though you know how vitally important it is to nurture your child, the world still hasn't figured it out. You may feel defensive about choosing to remain home with your child or guilty for trying to balance family and career.

There's no need for apology. No need for defensiveness. No need for guilt. There is, however, a great need for respect, support, and appreciation of motherhood. Nothing you have ever done or will ever do, no matter how grand, is more valuable.

Affirmation: Being a mom is an immensely valuable contribution.

SENSITIVITY

*Because I am a mother, I am capable of being
shocked: as I never was when I was not one.*
                    —*Margaret Atwood*

Being a mother increases your sensitivity. You're
painfully aware of the destruction of the environment, the instability of the economy, the crime
rate, the potential for war, the injustice and
suffering in the world.

"Watching the nightly news—reports of
murder, rape, political unrest—disturbs me far
more since Lynn was born," says the mother of
a six-month-old daughter. And no doubt mothers
all over the world shed tears as they watched the
heartbreaking scenes from the September 11,
2001, terrorist attacks.

You're shocked by pain, violence, and injustice
because you desperately want your child to grow
up in a safe world. It's imperative that you actively
work to create a safer, more peaceful world—
beginning with your own family.

**Affirmation: As a mother, I'm sensitive to the
suffering of the world.**

CAREER MOMS

We want daughters-in-law who are going to stay home and raise our grandchildren.

—Erma Bombeck

If you're a career mom, you may experience criticism, subtle or blatant, from mothers—perhaps even your own—who stayed at home with their children. You may hear comments such as, "Have you seen the latest studies on how children in day care are much more aggressive?" or "I don't know about you, but I make my family my number one priority."

Even if you assume these comments come from genuine concern for your child, it probably won't diminish your defensiveness. Even if you're perfectly confident of your decision, it's easy to feel undermined by another mother's judgments.

If such comments really grate on you, consider saying, "I appreciate your concern, but it would mean a great deal to me if you would support my decision to combine motherhood and a career." And take solace that you are doing the very best you can for your child and for yourself.

Affirmation: I don't need to defend my decision to balance career and family.

STAY-AT-HOME MOMS

*If the women's movement did any harm at all,
it gave the woman who stayed at home an
inferiority complex.*

—*Barbara Walters*

She's right. For all the crucial advances the
women's movement achieved, motherhood got
left behind. Feminists often portrayed it as a lowly,
second-rate trap, especially for the women who
put their careers on hold in order to care for their
children full-time.

Happily, more and more women now
acknowledge mothering as an area of expertise
and achievement. And hopefully, as more women
choose and are economically able to remain home
with their children, motherhood as a career will be
increasingly valued throughout society.

**Affirmation: Being a stay-at-home mom is a
highly respectable occupation.**

STICKINESS

*Even when freshly washed and relieved of all
obvious confections, children tend to be sticky.*
— Fran Lebowitz

Truer words were never spoken, literally and
figuratively. Children are sticky to pick up, sticky
to bring up.

Most moms agree that parenting requires
constant effort to work your way through sticky
situations. Today's sticky situation is cleaning up
the strained peas that end up everywhere but in
the baby's mouth. Tomorrow's sticky situation will
be answering questions like "Where do babies
come from?" and "Why are we here?"

Sometimes the sticky matter is obvious;
resolving it merely requires a warm bath. Other
times, what's sticky is trying to figure out what
your child really needs from you.

Affirmation: Parents face many sticky situations.

STAY-AT-HOME DADS

These guys, frontline soldiers on an unforgiving battlefield, still fight the expectations of what a dad's role in society is, and find, just like moms, the rewards are still worthwhile.

—Julian Orenstein

Stay-at-home dads are the parenting pioneers of the new millennium. It's a difficult role to play for many reasons.

One, men generally have relatively limited experience and cultural conditioning for child-raising. Two, even in today's society, men are often looked upon as breadwinners; some people view stay-at-home dads as slackers. Three, stay-at-home dads lack peers. Being so rare, stay-at-home dads aren't able to connect with a network of dads who share the same experiences.

If you head to the office while your partner takes care of your child at home, remember this: Stay-at-home dads need as much—if not more—support as stay-at-home moms do. Hopefully these early pioneers will blaze a trail, encouraging more and more fathers to care for their children in the years to come.

Affirmation: Stay-at-home dads are pioneers.

TEACHING

A child of one can be taught not to do certain things such as touch a hot stove, turn on the gas, pull lamps off their tables by their cords, or wake mommy before noon.

—Joan Rivers

Well, maybe that's asking a little much.

But you can teach a baby certain things that will make your life a little easier. For example, it's possible to teach your baby to remain in a playpen while you grab a quick shower or answer the phone. And it's possible to teach your baby to sleep at night, even if her internal clock has days and nights confused, so you're not up at all hours.

Caring for a baby is challenging. Whenever possible, teach your child lessons that will give you a much-needed respite.

Affirmation: There are ways to make my life easier.

STAYING CALM

The real menace in dealing with a five-year-old is that in no time at all you begin to sound like a five-year-old.

—Jean Kerr

And the real menace with dealing with a screaming newborn is that in no time at all you begin to sound like a screaming newborn, too.

When your child is upset, whining, or crying, it's natural to respond at the same level. As your patience wears thin, you lose perspective and find yourself in a screaming match that only makes things worse. No matter how hard you try to always act like the "designated adult," you sometimes lose your cool.

Here's where a "Mother's Time-Out" comes in handy. When you feel your temper and blood pressure start to rise, remove yourself, even if only for a few minutes. Take a deep breath. Count to ten. Remember that you're a perfectly reasonable adult. Have a good laugh at yourself, if it helps.

Gathering your wits and modulating your voice are the best ways to comfort your child and yourself.

Affirmation: I'll remember that I'm the adult here.

SPENDING

*If you want your children to turn out well,
spend twice as much time on them and half as
much money.*

—*Abigail Van Buren*

You may or may not be able to afford designer
overalls, gourmet baby food, and the top-of-the-
line stroller you admired from a distance at the
park. Unless you have infinite disposable income,
there will be times when you say to yourself or
to your child, "No. That's something we just
can't afford."

When that happens, don't for a minute think
you're depriving your child. If anything, you're
teaching him the value of money in an honest,
loving way.

Ultimately, the real treasures are your time,
attention, and affection. I have yet to meet
anyone who seriously complains that his or her
parents didn't buy him or her enough toys. But
I've met way too many people still suffering from
a shortage of their parents' love.

Affirmation: Love is priceless.

INDEPENDENCE

A mother is not a person to lean on but a person to make leaning unnecessary.
—Dorothy Canfield Fisher

Right now your baby's dependence on you is absolute. Your constant care is literally a matter of life and death.

But before long, your task will change. Little by little, you'll shift from fulfilling your child's every need to facilitating your child's independence.

Fostering your child's independence will be painful. It'll mean standing back so she may succeed on her own. When your baby begins to sit in a highchair and drink from a cup, you'll be challenged not to hover over her. When she takes her first steps, you'll have to let go and pray she won't fall, even if it's inevitable she will.

Right now, your baby needs your care. But every day you help her learn to care for herself.

Affirmation: I'll foster my baby's independence.

SANCTUARY

Children belong in families, which, ideally, serve as a sanctuary and a cushion from the world at large.

—Louise Hast

I know plenty of people who dread returning to their childhood homes, fearful of feeling alienated in the places where they should feel the greatest sense of belonging.

It doesn't have to be this way. And therein lies the hope. Pledge to make your home—the one you're building right now—a safe haven where your child is free to be himself. Make it a warm, friendly port where your child can seek comfort amid life's storms. Make it a sanctuary to which he'll always gladly return.

Affirmation: Our home is a sanctuary.

EMOTIONAL SECURITY

The future of the world would be assured if every child were loved.

—Bernie S. Siegel

What a difference it would make if all children felt secure, their physical and emotional needs consistently met by devoted, loving parents. Apathy, violence—everything from garden-variety rudeness to serious crime—might fade, or even disappear, if the world were filled with people who truly felt loved.

This may sound like a utopian vision, impossible to attain. But as the Talmudic saying goes, "Whoever saves a single soul, it is as if he had saved the entire world."

Affirmation: I'm helping secure the future.

FRIENDS

Hold a true friend with both your hands.
—Nigerian proverb

Being a new mother requires you to set aside many aspects of your life, including your friendships. You no longer have time to talk on the phone, go out for coffee, or attend dinner parties. When you do find a rare moment with your friends, you feel awkward, as if being a mother has changed the dynamics of your friendship.

A few casual friends may drift away during this time. Your true friends may drift away, too—unless you make an effort to hold them close. Make sure they know you still care for them deeply. Talk to them whenever you can, sharing your hopes and fears and ups and downs. Listen to them and make it a priority to take part in their lives, too.

Hold your friends with both hands and, more importantly, with all your heart.

Affirmation: I won't let my friends drift away.

IMITATION

Imitation is the sincerest flattery.
                    —*Charles Caleb Colton*

You love it when people say your baby looks exactly like you. You love it when she shows signs of being stubborn and determined—just like you. You love it when she jives with you to your favorite CD.

You know your child is an independent, unique individual, yet you're flattered by the many ways in which she imitates you. After all, she shares your genetic makeup, and she's socialized by your words and actions. Imitation is inevitable.

It's okay to be flattered by this imitation—as long as you also support the ways in which your baby differs from you. It's not as important to have a mini replica of yourself as it is to have a child who's comfortable with her own identity.

Affirmation: My baby doesn't have to be exactly like me.

SOLO PLAY

*She needs to learn that she can entertain herself,
so let her practice.*
—Glade B. Curtis and Judith Schuler

Years ago, we took our children to a friend's cabin on Madeline Island in Lake Superior. There was no TV, no VCR, no shopping mall to amuse and distract them.

Within an hour of unpacking, the kids disappeared much to our surprise. Later, they reappeared in makeshift costumes and proceeded to present a play. They spent the rest of the weekend quietly reading, collecting rocks, and playing word games.

That weekend taught me a lot about parenting. Left to their own devices, children—even babies— can often entertain themselves. You don't need to entertain your baby every waking hour. To encourage solo play, give your baby plenty of time alone with a few toys or with a good view of his surroundings. You'll be surprised at how content he'll be on his own.

Affirmation: I don't always need to entertain my child.

GENDER DIFFERENCES

*It is hard to raise sons; and much harder to
raise daughters.*

—Shalom Aleichem

The fact is, it's equally hard and equally satisfying
to raise sons and daughters. Neither is better or
worse, weaker or stronger, easier or harder.

Since I have one of each, I say sex is far less
important than personality. Boys are perceived as
"handfuls" because they tend to be extremely
active, but maybe Emma's mom never gets a
moment's rest because she's constantly chasing
after her daughter on the playground. Girls are
perceived as difficult because they tend to be
overly sensitive, but maybe Jake's mom needs to
frequently soothe him because the other children
at play group easily upset him.

Your baby's challenging traits may be gender
based, but they may also stem from your baby's
unique personality. Boys and girls are distinctly
different, but all babies are different from one
another regardless of sex.

**Affirmation: Boys and girls are equally hard
to raise.**

PERSONAL GROWTH

Parenthood is quite a long word. I expect it contains the rest of my life.

—Karen Scott Boates

You're not born with the feelings or the skills that are necessary to be a good mother. You have years—in fact, your whole lifetime—to become a better, more effective parent.

You learn from your mistakes, from reading and talking to other parents, and mostly from spending time getting to know your child. As you come to know your child—what each cry means, her likes and dislikes, her idiosyncrasies—you get better and better at giving her what she needs.

And as your skills grow, so does your love. With each passing year your child becomes dearer and dearer to you, and you become more confident in your ability to nurture and guide.

You're already a better parent than you were two weeks ago. And you'll be a better parent two months from now and two years from now. But that's only if you're willing to grow on the job.

Affirmation: I have the rest of my life to become the parent I want to be.

STAY-AT-HOME MOMS

You'll wake up some mornings and think, "How will I possibly get through this endless day within these four walls?"
—The Riverside Mothers Group

If you wake up one morning unable to face another day as a stay-at-home mom, pretend it's just another day at the office.

Grab your "coworker" and enjoy a little "water cooler talk" about the morning headlines and last night's prime-time fare. You can sip a cuppa decaf while he enjoys some milk or formula. Collaborate on the Pat-a-Cake project or the Dr. Seuss research until lunch time. After lunch, your coworker may log some billable napping hours, while you attend to phone calls and e-mails.

The whistle blows at five when the third employee walks in the door. Brief him on the day's progress of each project, then commute back "home," where you can get out of your work clothes and enjoy the evening.

Affirmation: A day of mothering is just like a day at the office.

EXPECTATIONS

Children are likely to live up to what you believe of them.

—*Lady Bird Johnson*

I once saw a child-development expert describe how he found his eighteen-month-old daughter perched precariously on the top of their swing set. Instead of shouting, "Be careful, you're going to fall!" he calmly repeated to her, "You have perfect balance. You have perfect balance."

His example is tough to follow. It's hard to stay cool when your child's about to fall and hurt herself physically or emotionally. Your natural instinct is to warn of imminent danger rather than encourage potential triumph.

But the real failure is not having the courage to let your child try. You give your child the critical gift of confidence when you respect her inner strength, resilience, and ability to rise to challenges.

Affirmation: I'll have faith in my child's abilities.

UNCONDITIONAL LOVE

*Adorable children are considered to be the
general property of the human race. (Rude
children belong to their mothers.)*

—*Judith Martin*

Many babies are adorable, cuddly, sweet,
precious, cute. They instantly charm everyone
who meets them, reducing utter strangers to
smiles and coos.

But some babies are fussy, rude, cantankerous,
and perhaps even—dare I say—ugly. No one coos
over them. These babies truly belong to their
mothers. More importantly, these babies prove
just how strong a mother's love can be.

It's easy to love a baby who looks and acts like
an angel sent from heaven above. But it takes
true devotion and patience to love a child who
looks and acts like an irritable alien dropped from
a distant planet.

If you have a baby "only a mother could love,"
realize that your love is unconditional. You love
your child despite his imperfections, and that's the
strongest love of all.

**Affirmation: My baby doesn't have to be
adorable for me to love him.**

VOCABULARY

The beginning of wisdom is to call things by their right names.

—Chinese proverb

It's not too early to begin introducing your child to the proper names for anatomy.

Although euphemisms abound—such as *private parts* for *penis* or *vagina*—many contemporary parents are opting for the right names right from the beginning. And studies suggest that children who learn correct vocabulary rather than euphemisms grow up more comfortable with their bodies, more candid and confident about their sexuality.

There's nothing to be squeamish or embarrassed about. Consider it part of your child's education.

Affirmation: I'll teach my child to be comfortable with all the parts of the body.

LULLABIES

They sang the way parents have always sung to their children…to lull them and soothe them…and, most of all, to drown them out.
—Sherril Jaffe

"Rock-a-bye baby, in the treetop…"

You serenade your child with the lullabies your parents sang to you as you drifted off to sleep. My mother-in-law crooned "The Sandman Song" to my children when they slept at her house, just as she once did to lull their father to sleep.

Sometimes a simple lullaby does the trick; other times your child needs another verse, a bedtime story, or a massage to calm her restlessness and help ease her into slumber. A musical mobile or night-light helps, too. But ultimately, nothing comforts your child like the sound of your voice singing to her from out of the dark.

Affirmation: Lullabies help my baby drift off to sleep.

DREAMS

My mother wanted me to be her wings, to fly as she never quite had the courage to do.

—Erica Jong

You must live your own life fully, rather than living through your child.

When you fail to fulfill your own aspirations, you consciously or unconsciously expect your child to realize your lost dreams and thwarted ambitions. The race you never ran, the book you never wrote, the acting career you never tried— these disappointments carry over to the next generation, and you hope your child will do everything you wanted to do.

Even as you begin mothering, you must re-commit to follow your own dreams so your child can follow his own.

Affirmation: I won't live through my child.

RAINY DAYS

Do not, on a rainy day, ask your child what he feels like doing, because I assure you that what he feels like doing, you won't feel like watching.
—*Fran Lebowitz*

Rainy days with babies can be a disaster or a delight, depending on your attitude. It's easy to feel frustrated when it's dreary outside and both you and your child are climbing the walls. You can suffer until the rain stops, or you can take this opportunity to tap your creativity.

Rainy days are perfect opportunities for art projects and puppet shows. You could even strap the baby in a Snugli, sing songs, and dance—all while doing some housecleaning. Or you could muster your spirit of adventure, pull on galoshes and ponchos, and go for a stroll in the puddles.

Motherhood relies on inventiveness in the face of adversity, so you can turn drizzly days into warm, memorable ones.

Affirmation: I'll use my imagination on rainy days.

BREAKS

The quickest way for a parent to get a child's attention is to sit down and look comfortable.
—Lane Olinghouse

Your child can be happily occupied as long as you're busy making beds or washing dishes, but the instant you call a friend or sit down to catch your breath, she's right in your face, begging for attention.

Here are a few strategies to keep your breaks relatively disturbance-free:

- Go into another room. Even a newborn can be secure in a bassinet while you steal a few moments in your bedroom or the bathroom.
- Be firm. Establish your right to privacy now, while your child is very young, so she'll take it in stride as she grows.
- Be creative. Find a distraction that will occupy her attention. Hand her a favorite toy or a switch on the mobile over her crib.

Affirmation: I won't be disturbed when I take my breaks.

A DAY IN THE LIFE

Just as you begin to nurse the baby, your six-year-old screams because the two-year-old took her toy. You firmly reprimand the two-year-old, who then begins to cry and tries to crawl in your lap. Having a new baby is difficult in itself, but how will you manage with so many kids?

If you're a veteran mother with older children and a new baby, you may find these first few months to be particularly stressful, especially when sibling rivalry flares up. You want to be fair, you want to keep the peace, and above all else you want each of your children to get what's needed.

Here's when situational ethics and artful negotiation enter into the equation. At any given moment, you need to make the best possible decision for everyone, including you. Sometimes the baby's needs prevail, sometimes the middle child needs attention while the older child entertains the baby, and sometimes you need to do whatever it takes to make it easier on yourself, which might mean calling the sitter.

Affirmation: Veteran moms can survive sibling rivalry.

DEVOTION

Your children are always your "babies," even if they have gray hair.

—Janet Leigh

You'll never, ever stop caring for and worrying about your child. The specifics simply change over time.

The intense care giving of early motherhood turns into the constant supervision of a toddler, which gives way to the mentoring of a school-age child, which evolves into the guiding of an adolescent as he begins the gradual journey into adulthood.

You're needed at each stage, only in different ways. At this early stage, your relationship is absolutely symbiotic. Gradually, you separate and increasingly care for your child from afar.

But no matter how old and gray your child gets (and you yourself will get plenty of gray hair in the process), you'll always be his mommy, and he'll always be your "baby."

Affirmation: Motherhood is forever.

DRIVING

A suburban mother's role is to deliver children obstetrically once, and by car forever after.
—Peter De Vries

Some of the nicest times with your child may very well take place while driving in your car.

For one thing, the baby is captive; you're assured she's not about to crawl into the garbage or tumble down the stairs. And as most moms learn, driving is often the best way to lull a newborn. (I've known more than one mother who drove up and down her driveway just to get her baby to sleep.)

When your child is older, you may have some of the best, most spontaneous conversations in transit. "What does the tooth fairy do with the teeth?" and "Where does the sky stop?" are some of the topics I've been treated to over the years.

Like many journeys, driving with a baby can be frustrating or fun. It all depends on how you navigate the course.

Affirmation: I'll make the most of our time in the car.

CHALLENGES

A woman who can cope with the terrible twos can cope with anything.

—Judith Clabes

And a woman who can cope with labor and delivery can cope with anything. And a woman who can cope with getting up all night with a newborn can cope with anything. And a woman who can cope with chasing after a baby can cope with anything.

Although you may dread the "terrible twos," which have an especially rough reputation, know that there are intense challenges at every juncture of motherhood. The stamina, patience, and inner peace required to raise your baby from age two to three are no more, no less than what's needed from conception to birth, from birth to age one, and from age one to two.

At each stage, you learn how much you are capable of. And at each stage, you stretch a little more.

Affirmation: I'm up to the task.

BEDTIME

The best time for parents to put the children to bed is while they still have the strength.
—Homer Phillips

Whether you put your child to bed on a strict schedule, keep him up till he drops, or something in between, the point is to keep bedtime from becoming a battle between an exhausted child and an equally exhausted adult.

One thing I've learned: Develop a bedtime routine and start it at the same time every night— at least forty-five minutes before your baby should be asleep. That gives you extra time for lullabies, last-minute diaper changes and feedings, bedtime stories, and those terribly important kisses that can only take place just when it's time to tuck 'em in.

Affirmation: I'll make bedtime as easy as possible.

OUTDOORS

Always keep your eyes on your baby. It takes one moment to crawl out of sight…right into (chose one): (a) the mudhole, (b) poison ivy, (c) the bee hive, (d) broken glass, (e) dog poop.
—Julian Orenstein

Your baby loves to play in the back yard or the park, but you're worried about the many dangers lying in wait for your unsuspecting baby: poison ivy, bugs, litter, all sorts of animal droppings.

Although playing outdoors isn't as safe as playing inside a baby-proofed house, a back yard or a park offers terrific opportunities for your baby to explore the world.

To ease some of your fears, take a moment to survey an outdoor area before you give your baby free rein. And know that nearly every baby has eaten dirt, chewed on grass, and covered herself in mud—and survived.

Affirmation: I'll use common sense when my baby plays outdoors.

A DAY IN THE LIFE

You've been back to work for a few months, and your boss offered you a promotion. You're torn. It's the opportunity you've worked your whole career for, but it'll mean working harder and later. Will being a mother force you to pass up this chance for advancement?

It's hard enough to return to your regular job after having a baby. But attempting to be a good mother and to successfully advance your career is a tremendous challenge.

Before you accept this promotion, make sure you have the following things in your "survival kit":

- Child care you feel absolutely secure with—perhaps even on-site care
- Help from your partner or family and friends
- A contract spelling out the commitments and limitations of your new position
- A support network of career moms
- Patience

Being a mother shouldn't stop you from advancing your career. You just need to take steps to ensure that your family and career are equally successful.

Affirmation: I can succeed as a mother and advance my career.

LEGACIES

Nearly every day an echo of my mother's mothering wafts by me, like the aroma of soup simmering on a stove down the street.

—Anna Quindlen

Your mother's words ring in your ears. Perhaps you even catch yourself repeating them to your child.

It's eerie to find yourself sounding like your mother, especially now that you're a mother, too. You hear her words in a new context. You realize some of her mothering was wonderful, worthy of following. But you also realize that in other ways you'd prefer to forge a new path, free of her influence, truer to your own values and beliefs.

Whether you emulate her or veer from her example, your mother is your first role model, and her words and actions will continue to influence your new life as a mother.

Affirmation: Here are three positive things I learned from my mother:

1. _____

2. _____

3. _____

READING

Richer than I you can never be—
I had a Mother who read to me.
                              —Strickland W. Gillian

There are very few things in this world that are more valuable, more magical, more tender than holding your child in your arms, snuggling close, and reading him a story.

Your baby loves the sound of your voice, whether it's dramatic and full of silly sound effects or low, even, and almost hushed. Although he's too young to understand every word, he loves to hear tales of people, places, and things that will live in his imagination all the days of his life.

For those few moments, you and your baby enter a world all your own. When he's older, he'll ask for just *one more* story or just a *few more* pages, trying to stay in that wonderful world for as long as he can.

Read to your child every day, several times a day. It's one of the most wonderful gifts a mother and child can share.

Affirmation: It's magical when I read to my child.

BABY-PROOFING

You can disarm the coffee table by clearing off the top and taping foam rubber padding 'round the sharp edges...this style is known as "Infant Provincial."

—Peter Mayle

If your baby is mobile—or even edging toward the furniture—it's time to baby-proof.

Some parents' idea of baby-proofing is shrieking "No!" every time their children come within reaching distance of precious or dangerous objects. Not the best approach. This is one situation in which it's wiser to adapt the environment to the child.

For one thing, you'll get hoarse constantly screaming no. For another thing, it can't help but make your child feel bad about doing exactly what she should be doing at this stage—exploring the world relatively freely. And because screaming no doesn't always work, your valuables are much safer on a high shelf than within your baby's reach. Likewise, your baby is much safer when dangerous items are out of her grasp.

Affirmation: Baby-proofing is good protection all around.

ILLNESS

Diagnosis According to a Mother Mind:
Child has a runny nose...brain tumor
Child has a headache...brain tumor
Child has a funny spot on arm...arm tumor
                                    —Amy Krouse Rosenthal

Everything and anything seems like a life-threatening tragedy when your baby isn't feeling well. You diagnose the most outrageous ailments: tumors, German measles, whooping cough, cat scratch fever.

There are two ways to avoid jumping to such dire conclusions. One, educate yourself. Study a reputable guide to childhood health issues and learn to detect symptoms. You should always leave the final diagnosis to a pediatrician, but if you're familiar with certain ailments, you can keep your imagination from running wild.

Two, stay calm. It's easier said than done, but you need to keep a level head so you can rationally determine if your baby's simply under the weather or if he needs medical attention.

Affirmation: I'll educate myself and stay calm when my baby is sick.

SINGING

Don't worry if you can't carry a tune—little babies are notoriously undiscriminating when it comes to music.
> —Arlene Eisenberg, Heidi E. Murkoff,
> and Sandee E. Hathaway

It doesn't matter if you once got booed off the stage at a karaoke bar. It doesn't matter if your grade school choir teacher put you in charge of opening and closing the curtains so you wouldn't actually sing at the recital. It doesn't matter if people cringe when you sing along with the national anthem at ball games. None of it matters because your baby loves to hear you sing.

So grab your baby and dance around the house, belting out every nursery rhyme you know. You don't know any nursery rhymes? Then sing your favorite pop songs. Don't know the lyrics? Make them up!

Set all your inhibitions aside and just sing. Your baby loves the sound of your voice with all its highs, lows, and in betweens. More importantly, your baby loves it when you pull out all the stops just for her.

Affirmation: I'll set my inhibitions aside and sing for my baby.

FEEDING

A man finds out what is meant by a spitting image when he tries to feed cereal to his infant.
—*Imogene Fey*

Simma, the nineteen-year-old who cared for Zoe when she was an infant, still talks about the Gerber's squash—squishy, orange-colored mush—that dripped down her clothes after feeding Zoe one morning.

Feeding a baby is a mess! Yet you take pleasure and pride with each spoonful of ground, puréed, and strained food your child eats—and spits out. And as he graduates from baby carrots to junior chicken with vegetables, you congratulate him for his growth. You congratulate yourself for your patience and mostly for the relief that, little by little, there's more ending up in the mouth than on the floor.

Affirmation: My child is worth the mess.

NATURE

*In a world that is cutting down its trees to build
highways, losing its earth to concrete, babies
are almost the only remaining link with nature,
with the natural world of living things from which
we spring.*

—Eda J. Leshan

At times, the world seems nothing more than an
endless, lifeless sea of concrete. It's easy to feel far
removed from nature, especially if you live in the
city. Having a baby brings you closer to that
natural world.

   In the natural world, plants and tress are born,
breathe, feed, grow, and exist only to bear off-
spring, to create new life. You, too, have created
a new life, and your baby will breathe, feed, grow,
and may someday create a new life as well.

   To sanctify your connection to the natural world,
plant a tree in your yard or in a park. As you
watch both the tree and your baby grow, you'll
be reminded of your place in the circle of life.

**Affirmation: Having a baby brings me closer
to nature.**

SENSUALITY

*I think when my children are gone I'll have to
have beautiful fabrics to wear and sleep and sit
on...to endure the sensual deprivation of my
warm living babies.*

—Nancy Thayer

One tangible tradeoff for the hard work of caring
for a new baby is the pleasure of cuddling, rocking, holding her closely against your own skin.

Although my children still grant me occasional
hugs, gone are the days of rocking them for hours,
luxuriating in their silky softness, breathing in their
warm fragrance.

You should appreciate this physical intimacy
now. Once your child grows older, you'll find
yourself begging new moms for the privilege of
holding their babies. Oh! Just a moment or two
to bathe again in that singular, sensual delight.

**Affirmation: I appreciate the pleasure of holding
my baby.**

RECOGNITION

In the job of home keeping there is no raise from the boss and seldom praise from others to show us that we've hit the mark.
                                    —Anne Morrow Lindbergh

The same is true of motherhood.

Our society gives little recognition for motherhood—no paycheck, no performance reviews or bonuses, and hardly a word of praise on what a fabulous job you're doing.

We must all work together to give motherhood the recognition it deserves. Here's one way to start: Each time you notice a mother doing something well—such as being especially patient, understanding, or creative—make a point to say something positive. For yourself, keep a journal or a chart to note your parenting high points. Each time you do something you're especially proud of, reward yourself with a small gift, an hour-long bath, or anything that helps you commemorate a job well done.

Affirmation: I'm doing a great job!

REVELATION

If there were no other reasons, this alone would be the value of children: the way they reveal you to yourself.

—Elizabeth Berg

As you struggle to meet your expectations of motherhood, you learn about your strengths and weaknesses.

When you walk up and down the hall for hours on end, soothing your sick baby, you realize how compassionate you are. Likewise, when you get angry because it takes thirty minutes to load the diaper bag, you realize you need to be more organized.

Being a mother reveals so much about you. With this self-knowledge, you can celebrate your strengths and improve your weaknesses.

Affirmation: I'm learning so much about myself.

PATIENCE

Everything about a new family takes time.
—Judy Blume

If you were starting a new job, you'd likely give yourself at least a few weeks—if not months—to learn your new duties, to understand office politics, to find a productive routine and a rhythm. You bring home a new baby, however, and you expect everything to run smoothly from day one.

This is an incredibly unrealistic expectation! It takes days, sometimes weeks, to learn how to nourish and comfort a newborn. It takes weeks, sometimes months, to figure out how to integrate your new responsibilities as a parent with your previous demands in and out of the home. It takes months, sometimes years, to make the complete shift from being a couple to being parents, to being a family.

Take your time. Gradually, everything will fall into place.

Affirmation: I don't have to have it all figured out today.

HONESTY

The first time I lied to my baby, I told him that it was his face on the baby food jar.
—Maxine Chernoff

The first time I lied to Zoe, I told her she needed a nap because she was tired. Then I caught myself, retracted my statement, and told her the truth: "You need a nap because *I'm* tired."

Even though your baby isn't old enough to understand much of what you're saying, it's never too early to grapple with the complexities of honesty. Will you tell convenient white lies today and in the years to come? Will you insist that the tooth fairy is real, only to have your child someday discover a half-dozen teeth wrapped in toilet paper at the bottom of your sweater drawer? Will you be honest about the death of a grandparent, the loss of a job, an illness? Will you be as open and honest as your child can manage, or will you shield him from the truth?

More and more, parents choose to be honest with their children. It's a good philosophy, especially if you want your child to be honest with you.

Affirmation: I'll be honest with my child.

GRANDPARENTS

You feel completely comfortable entrusting your baby to [them] for long periods of time, which is why most grandparents flee to Florida at the earliest opportunity.

—Dave Barry

Some grandparents beg to take regular shifts, some are just on call, and some say, "I've done my time. Don't expect me to baby-sit."

If your child's grandparents live close by and are eager to baby-sit once in a while, count yourself lucky for two reasons: The grandparents can have the pleasure of getting to know their grandchild; and you can relax while you're out because your baby will be with people who love her almost as much as you do.

But if the grandparents are less than eager to baby-sit, you need to respect their decision. Don't guilt them into baby-sitting or dump the baby on them without their okay. There are other ways they can bond with their grandchild, when they want to.

Affirmation: I'll respect the grandparents' decision when it comes to baby-sitting.

A DAY IN THE LIFE

You've been going since six, when the baby woke with an earache. You've made trips to the pediatrician's and the drugstore, burned some brownies, and fielded four calls from your mother, and the baby still hasn't napped. Your husband saunters in at six o'clock and innocently says, "Boy, did I have a hard day at work! What did you do all day?"

Before you throw the baby—and everything else in sight—at him, take a deep breath and count to ten.

Maybe he doesn't know how hard you work. If he hasn't tried it, he probably doesn't comprehend how exhausting a job you have. That doesn't mean you need to throw a tantrum or go on strike to get your message across. Simply describe the details of your day without embellishing or diminishing how hard you work and how much you do.

And maybe he did have a hard day, just as hard as yours. Tell each other about your days as you make supper and look after the baby together. This isn't time to one-up each other, but time to support each other for the contributions you make to your family.

Affirmation: We both have hard days.

LITTLE THINGS

All day I did the little things, the little things that do not show.

—Blanche Ban Kudee

"What did you do today?" I asked my friend Maggie, mother of three.

"Not much," Maggie replied. "I made pancakes for breakfast, darned socks, designed two Halloween costumes, drove Abe to piano lessons, got groceries, took Sophie to the pediatrician, vacuumed, planted bulbs in the garden, made egg rolls for dinner, and read five books to Elly."

Oh, that's all.

You may call them "little things," but every mother makes many small yet invaluable contributions to her family each day.

If you feel your time isn't valuable or well spent, try this experiment: At the end of each day this week, write down everything you've accomplished as a mom—whether you're a career mom or a stay-at-home mom. Include everything. At the end of the week, look at your list and ask, "How big a difference am I making?"

Affirmation: The "little things" make a huge difference.

HUMOR

As a final bequest I would like to leave my children with a sense of humor. Living with them has improved mine.

—*Phyllis Theroux*

A sharpened sense of humor is one of the side benefits of motherhood. You cultivate it out of necessity; it serves you well in those moments when you don't know whether to burst out laughing or burst into tears.

It's a great advantage to be able to laugh when your baby skips both naps, then finally falls asleep the minute the baby sitter arrives, or when he grins gleefully after emptying your entire sock drawer.

Seeing the humor in life keeps things in perspective. Humor is the all-important quality that separates mothers who lose it from mothers who make it.

Affirmation: I'll have a sense of humor.

ROLE MODELS

Children have never been very good at listening to their elders, but they have never failed to imitate them.

—*James Baldwin*

Too often parents are guilty of "Do what I say, not what I do." Yet as James Baldwin points out, your child is much more likely to emulate your behavior than follow your words.

Your child is watching you, aware of your choices, sensitive to the disparity between your actions and your advice—even at this young age. And as she grows, you can't expect her to be athletic if you watch TV all night long with a bag of chips in your lap. Nor will she learn to clean up her room if you can't keep your own belongings in order.

If you're to be an effective role model, your words and deeds must match. You must do as you say if you want your child to do the same.

Affirmation: I'll set a consistent example.

CRAWLING

For the first six months or so, your opponent has been unable to escape. Alas, the rules are about to change drastically…The enemy is now mobile.
—Peter Mayle

Crawling! When your baby can scoot around on all fours, it's time to rearrange the furniture, remove fragile objects, and prepare to be on guard duty every second of the day.

You don't realize how easy you had it until your baby starts to crawl. Before, you could keep track of him, now he's halfway across the living room, about to pull the lamp down on his head. You used to be able to answer the phone, fix dinner, even take a shower in peace; now you can't turn your back for a second, and you desperately wish you had eyes in the back of your head.

Like every milestone, it's a blessing and a curse. You celebrate each step forward and rise to the occasion.

Affirmation: It's a whole new ball game.

COMMITMENT

I am seeking, I am striving, I am in it with all my heart.

—*Vincent van Gogh*

You seek the knowledge, the wisdom, the patience to guide your child through every step of this journey.

You strive to be the very best parent you can possibly be, knowing you are still learning, still growing, still striving to understand what it means to be a mother.

You fully commit to the responsibilities of parenthood. Love and good intentions are all you need as you continue to try to be the very best mother you know how to be.

Affirmation: I am in it with all my heart.

SINGLE MOMS

I'm a single mother. When I say that I say it with Pride, Humility, Strength, Fear, Gratefulness and Honor. Kind of an odd mixture of feelings, wouldn't you say?

—Kathleen Driggers

Raising a child is a tough job for two parents sharing the load; it's an awesome task for one parent to take on. If you're a single mom, you most likely feel proud and humble, strong and weak.

But during the times when your complex emotions are too much to bear, seek support. Turn to your family and friends to look after the baby while you take a break. Join a support group with single moms who can sympathize with your feelings and experiences.

Don't be ashamed of your mixed emotions. Just know that getting support will help you stay as emotionally balanced as possible.

Affirmation: Being a single mom is a complex job with complex emotions.

BABY

Oh, baby, baby, baby dear.

—E. Nesbit

Think for a moment about the word *baby*. People call their sweethearts "baby," their cars "baby," their pets "baby." It's a loving term of endearment.

But people also use baby as an insult. If you're a "baby," you're immature and juvenile. More specifically, a "big baby" is someone who is overly timid and difficult. A "crybaby" whimpers and snivels at the drop of hat.

Still yet, baby is a verb. To "baby" is to spoil, overindulge, coddle, pamper.

If you had to form a comprehensive definition for the word *baby*, it might be this: A baby is something or someone that—despite being juvenile, difficult, and whimpering—is often pampered and dearly loved.

Affirmation: Let me call you "baby."

INVENTIVENESS

Well, another year has gone by and still the Nobel Prize has not yet been awarded to the inventor of the Snugli baby carrier. I can't figure it.

—Anna Quindlen

Neither can I.

But whoever came up with this brilliant idea unquestionably deserves some prestigious award or at least the thanks of mothers everywhere.

I myself am thankful to the inventors of silent push toys, collapsible strollers, and glow-in-the-dark pacifiers.

They say necessity is the mother of invention. I'm glad there are inventors out there who know what's necessary to make a mother's life easier.

Affirmation: I'd like to thank the inventor of

_____.

CEREAL

My life is filled with cereal.

—Phyllis McGinley

Rice cereal, oatmeal, Froot Loops with toys in the box—cereal is a great metaphor for parenting.

Cereal is comforting, as is the nurturing relationship between a parent and a child. And most cereal is sweet; even the healthiest granola has an element of sweetness, not unlike the sweetness you feel as you sit across the kitchen table from your child.

And in its own way, cereal is a yardstick for your child's growth and independence. When it's time to introduce solids, you feed her rice cereal. One of her first finger foods is Cheerios. And by the time your child is five or six, she can tear into the Wheaties box and add the milk herself.

But don't get too excited. It generally takes ten more years before she'll put the box back in the cupboard without being told.

Affirmation: Cereal is a perfect metaphor for parenthood.

PLAYFULNESS

Adults are obsolete children.

—*Dr. Seuss*

It's easy to lose your childlike spirit when you're burdened with work, bills, and other demands of adult life. Here's one way that your child can be your teacher: Simply being with your child reawakens the magical energy that lies within you.

Reading *The Cat in the Hat* and other beloved Dr. Seuss classics to your child helps you remember how to be spontaneous, goofy, and playful. So does making up whimsical rhymes, spinning in circles, being silly just for the sake of being silly, and wondering how many dandelions are populating the front yard.

Being a kid at heart renews your spirit when the adult world seems overwhelming. It restores your energy and makes it easier to handle all your adult concerns.

Affirmation: Being a parent reawakens my childlike spirit.

CHANGES

*Every day you wake up to discover a slightly
different person sleeping in that cradle, that crib,
that bottom bunk, that distant sleeping bag.*
—Joyce Maynard

Watching your child grow is a bittersweet mix of
anticipation and loss.

As you witness your tiny newborn emerge from
her sleepy cocoon and transform from a cuddly
baby into an active toddler, and then into an
inquisitive child, you'll both celebrate and grieve.
Even now, you're thrilled by each new leap, yet
painfully aware that time races on.

Not that you would stop it. You welcome your
child's growth and strive to savor every moment
of every passing day.

Affirmation: I celebrate my child's growth.

DIPLOMACY

My evolution into a politician developed not in opposition to my role as a mother, but as an extension of it.

—Madeleine Kunin

As a mother, you have the qualities of a savvy politician. You're a master negotiator and an expert peacemaker, and you're totally committed to the concerns of your constituency.

The skills you gain in motherhood apply to other parts of life. You become a better listener and are able to read between the lines, which enhances your communication in every relationship. You learn to facilitate, moderate, legislate, and govern with care and respect—useful skills for creating a healthy family as well as a peaceful world.

Affirmation: Motherhood is filled with transferable skills.

GRANDPARENTS

A mother becomes a true grandmother the day she stops noticing the terrible things her children do because she is so enchanted with the wonderful things her grandchildren do.

—Lois Wyse

Now that you're a mother, you have a great opportunity to heal or cement the relationship between you and your parents or your in-laws.

For starters, you now have something wonderful in common—your love for the baby. You now have motivation to visit or keep in touch on a regular basis. And even if unfinished business remains between you, your parents or in-laws can't help but adore your child and respect you for producing such a miracle.

As your parents and in-laws develop a relationship with their grandchild, take this opportunity to strengthen your relationship with them.

Affirmation: I'll strengthen my relationship with my parents and in-laws.

MIRACLE

This is the real creation: not the accident of childbirth, but the miracle of man-birth and woman-birth.

—D. H. Lawrence

While you were pregnant, you felt as if you were privy to a miracle. Conceiving your child, helping her grow in your womb, giving birth—it was a divine, miraculous event.

But the miracle did not end when you delivered your baby. The real miracle is how you and your partner have been transformed from woman and man to mother and father. Your daily life has changed, your perspective has changed, your identity has changed, your purpose and goals have changed.

Having a baby is a metamorphosis, one that fills you with wonder and amazement. It's a miracle.

Affirmation: Becoming a mother and a father is a miracle.

UPS AND DOWNS

This mother needs happy, reputable children, and that one needs unhappy ones: otherwise she cannot show her kindness as a mother.
—*Friedrich Nietzsche*

Some mothers are happy only when their children are happy. The moment their children have a problem, they can't handle the pressure. Other mothers thrive on problems and pressure. They simply don't feel purposeful unless they're mending their children's crises.

Neither is a healthy model for motherhood. Starting today, make a conscious effort to avoid both. Instead, develop inner strength so you can confront problems and also develop inner peace so you can take satisfaction in your baby's happiness.

Over the years, your child will have ups, downs, and many in-betweens. If you react only to the ups or only to the downs, you'll miss some of the sweetest moments of motherhood.

Affirmation: I'll cultivate inner strength and inner peace.

ACCOMPLISHMENTS

One never notices what has been done; one can only see what remains to be done.

—Marie Curie

Today, you need to wash the dishes, scoop out the litter box, defrost the chicken, bathe the baby, and mail the bills. In the next few weeks, months, and years, you need to look for day care closer to work, lose fifteen pounds, save money for a college fund, build a deck on the house, and plan your dream vacation to Europe. No wonder you're stressed-out!

Try a change of perspective. Instead of looking at what remains to be done, look at what you have already accomplished. What did you do today? What have you done in the past few weeks, months, and years?

You may be surprised that what you've accomplished outweighs what you still want to accomplish. So instead of feeling stressed-out about what's on your to-do list, feel proud of how much you really get done.

Affirmation: I'll focus on my accomplishments, not just on what's left to do.

REALITY

We say that a girl with her doll anticipates the mother. It is more true, perhaps, that most mothers are still but children with playthings.
—F. H. Bradley

At times, it's easy to feel like a little girl playing make-believe with her adorable little doll. It's as if you're dressing your doll, feeding your doll, changing your doll's diaper.

But it can be quite frustrating when real life differs from make-believe. You can't just take the batteries out when your baby's wailing at two in the morning. You can't just set your baby back in the closet when you want to go to a friend's house or to work. You can't just return your baby to the store when he gets sick and seems "broken."

Your baby isn't a plaything, even if he seems that way sometimes. It's best to leave the world of make-believe to little girls, because being a mother requires you to stay grounded in reality.

Affirmation: My baby isn't a doll.

DIAPERS

Just when you're getting bored with changing diapers, another surprise turns up in one.
—*Arlene Eisenberg, Heidi E. Murkoff,
and Sandee E. Hathaway*

You might have been squeamish changing those first few dirty diapers. It's one of the less desirable duties of parenthood, and it takes time for new parents to get used to the sights and smells.

But just when you think you've steeled your stomach, seen the worst of the worst, and had it all under control...your baby starts eating solids.

Your baby's diaper deposits are now thicker, darker, and unfortunately smellier than they were when she was fed exclusively breast milk or formula. The diaper contents often take on the color of the latest meal—in some cases, they look exactly like the latest meal.

Your stomach may churn for a few days, but you'll adjust to this, too. You'll learn to take each new shocking discovery in stride.

Affirmation: I'll get used to changing diapers.

RISKS

*I love it when people say, "You can't do that."
It's like hearing "I dare you."*

—SARK

Sometimes you make parenting choices that are risky, that go against the grain, that raise the eyebrows of other parents in your day care or neighborhood.

One woman recalls the time she encouraged her kids—all under the age of five—to run naked around the back yard in the middle of a thunderstorm, much to her neighbors' surprise. Another describes how she "mainstreamed" her child who is autistic, despite all the experts, friends, and relatives who cautioned her against it.

When it comes to parenting, "you can't do it" is synonymous with "I wouldn't do it" or "I'm afraid of what will happen if you do it." But even the most well-meaning caution must be weighed against your own sense of what's right for your child. You must dare—even in the face of criticism—to trust your instincts and follow your heart.

Affirmation: I'll follow my heart and make my own parenting decisions.

MISTAKES

Mistakes are the portals of discovery.

—James Joyce

Your baby screams and screams until you realize the bottle's nipple is clogged, and he isn't getting any milk. You forget to pack extra diapers when you go to the park, so your baby has to stay in a wet diaper until you get home.

Every parent makes mistakes. Lots of them.

You can let mistakes fill you with guilt, or you can take them seriously but in stride. Mistakes are lessons. Each time you blow it—and you will—you discover how you can improve, and you can commit to try harder.

Affirmation: I'm learning from my mistakes.

SELF-PERCEPTION

Few things delight a baby more than her reflection.
—Penny Warner

It's a special moment when your baby first realizes that the baby in the mirror is really herself. She'll smile, reach out and touch her reflection, and giggle with delight. It's self-esteem, self-love, and self-acceptance in its purest and most joyous form.

As your child grows, her self-perception will be influenced—positively and negatively—by others. As writer Anaïs Nin says, "She lives on the reflections of herself in the eyes of others."

For now, however, set your baby in front of the mirror, and let her enjoy her delightful self. The more she comes to know her true reflection, the less likely she'll be to rely on others' reflections of her.

Affirmation: My baby's developing a sense of self.

MOTHER'S DAY

Unpleasant questions are being raised about Mother's Day. Is this day necessary?
—Russell Baker

The official "Hallmark" holiday reminds us to set aside one day of the year to formally honor mothers. But now that you're a mother, you probably could use a little honoring every day.

Next time you feel overwhelmed or unappreciated, take a step back and try to notice how your child honors you. Your baby may not be able to say "I love you" or make you a card with glitter and crayons, but he can give you a toothless smile, a burst of giggles, or a warm cuddle. Your baby lets you know how important you are when he stops crying the moment you pick him up, or when he smiles and kicks his legs when you walk into the room.

Your child loves, honors, and appreciates you. It doesn't have to be Mother's Day for you to notice how much you mean to your child.

Affirmation: Every day is Mother's Day.

EDUCATION

The best academy, a mother's knee.
—James Russell Lowell

In time, you'll send your child off to preschool, kindergarten, and someday, college. You may feel as if her education is in other people's hands.

But you'll always be your child's first and most influential teacher. You teach your child how to walk, talk, and feed herself. Not to mention that you teach your child values, the power of a hug, and how to make the world a cleaner, safer place.

No matter what she'll learn in school, what she learns from you is the foundation of her education.

Affirmation: I'm my child's best teacher.

FOOD

Whatever you do, don't let mealtime become battle time.

> —Arlene Eisenberg, Heidi E. Murkoff,
> and Sandee E. Hathaway

While you should care about what, when, and how much your child eats, you must be careful not to put too much emphasis on food.

Using food as a reward, insisting he swallow food that makes him gag, or pressuring him to eat when he's not hungry can lead to unnecessary power struggles. In some extreme cases, it can lead to eating disorders.

Food is one area in which it's important to be picky—about your battles, that is. Nourishment is essential, but what your child actually needs and what you think he needs are not always the same.

Affirmation: I'll choose my battles when it comes to food.

SELF-ESTEEM

I'm searching for my inner child.

—*Anonymous*

There was so much written in the late 1990s about the "inner child." This term usually refers to the child inside each of us, who in many cases is wounded and needs to recover self-esteem.

Think about your inner child. Does she have a healthy or unhealthy self-esteem? Does she feel loved? Wounded? Now imagine your own child as an adult. What type of inner child would you like her to have?

As a parent, you have great power to help your child develop healthy self-esteem. If you treat your child with respect and support her feelings, you can help her become an adult who feels loved, confident, and at peace with the world—and with her inner child.

Affirmation: I'll help my child develop a healthy self-esteem.

EXPENSES

It costs more now to amuse a child than it once did to educate his father.

—Vaughan Monroe

The other day I happened to walk into FAO Schwarz at the Mall of America near Minneapolis. Among the toys were a miniature car that a child can drive, a designer dollhouse, and a five-foot-tall plush gorilla.

Whatever happened to a teddy bear and a box of Crayola crayons? The cost of amusing a child is outrageous, far beyond what the average parent can or should have to afford.

Commercials want you to believe that your child requires lavish toys to be entertained. Fact is, he doesn't. You have the choice and the responsibility to resist going overboard. Simple toys—blocks, books, and even pots and pans—can amuse your child and keep you out of debt.

Affirmation: I won't spend a fortune on toys.

TEENAGERS

A baby-sitter is a teenager who comes in to act like an adult while the adults go out and act like teenagers.

—Harry Marsh

You don't mind leaving your baby with the mom next door, but leaving her with a teenager is especially hard. You imagine the sitter will tune out the baby while he or she talks on the phone… or forages through your closet…or invites friends over for a wild party.

How can you possibly enjoy yourself? You may as well just stay home.

Wrong! It's important to get out, even for a few hours and even if the sitter is barely old enough to drive. Chances are, your sitter comes highly recommended by other parents in your neighborhood and has lots of experience.

So go ahead. Go out and act like a teen again. Cruising with your partner, hanging out with friends, or window-shopping at the mall will reenergize and refresh you. It'll make you a better parent. It'll remind you that you still have a life!

Affirmation: I'll trust a sitter when I need a night out.

A DAY IN THE LIFE

Most of the babies in your play group are crawling or at least sitting up, while your Michael just rocks on his tummy. And he's one of the oldest! You don't mean to compare him to the others, but you're a little worried that something's wrong.

It's natural to compare your baby's development with other babies' and to worry when he doesn't appear to measure up.

In reality, babies develop at different rates. Some sit up at four months, while others need to be propped up past their six-month mark. Some babies are early crawlers, and some skip crawling altogether and at some point just get up and walk.

It wouldn't hurt to take your child in for a checkup. If everything is okay—which it probably is—try to stop worrying. Allow him to grow at his own rate, in his own unique way. In the meantime, watch for his individual progress. Start now by noticing one thing your child can do today that he couldn't do a week ago.

Affirmation: This week my child learned to

_____.

TEETHING

Adam and Eve had many advantages, but the principal one was that they escaped teething.
—Mark Twain

Babies usually begin teething somewhere between four and seven months, though it can begin anywhere from three months to one year. You feel so helpless watching your baby drool and fret as each new tooth pushes through the surface. As in most other areas of mothering, it's impossible to prevent the pain. All you can do is ease her suffering, knowing it's a necessary part of growth.

Meanwhile, teething rings, zwieback crackers, cold washcloths, and gum massages help. So does holding and rocking your baby, comforting her any way you can.

Affirmation: Teething is a necessary growing pain.

FLEXIBILITY

Never give in!

—*Winston Churchill*

Knowing when to stand firm in your decisions and when to be flexible is a constant challenge of good, responsible parenting.

While you want your child to respect your authority and consistency, you must also be aware that sometimes the situation requires flexibility. If you're usually firm about no naps after five o'clock, you might want to reconsider if your child seems irritable and exhausted. If, however, your baby is simply pushing the limits, you must have the wherewithal to stand your ground.

Consistency and flexibility are both necessary. Both require humility and wisdom.

Affirmation: I'll know when to be firm and when to be flexible.

SEPARATION

There is no fear as great in a small child as that of being left alone.

—T. Berry Brazelton

When the sitter arrives, you kiss the baby good-bye and then are completely undone as the baby bursts into inconsolable sobs, reaching for you as if he's being abandoned forever.

It's horrible to leave when your child's crying. But go you must. I used to force myself out the door with Zoe's screams echoing behind me, drive two blocks to the SuperAmerica, and call the sitter to make sure the crying had stopped. (It often had; ironically, my separation calmed her separation anxiety.)

How can you make separation anxiety easier? Never sneak out; this only confuses your child and exacerbates the fear. Leave a favorite teddy bear or blanket, or act out a ritual before you go. (I still kiss my children on a certain place that they can rub while I'm away.) And call home if it reassures you.

Little by little, your child will come to trust that you'll always return when you leave.

Affirmation: My baby and I can overcome separation anxiety.

MESSES

One of the most important things to remember about infant care is: Never change diapers in midstream.

—Don Marquis

Face it. There isn't a parent anywhere who hasn't been spit up on, peed on, or showered with half-digested food.

Although you know you're always in the line of fire, you can't predict when the attack will come. (It's usually right after you've changed into your best clothes, ready to walk out the door to a special event.)

Babies are messy, which is why most new moms live in their oldest, shabbiest sweatshirts. Consider it an occupational hazard. Save it as a "war story" to laugh about when the perpetrator is grown.

Affirmation: I'll expect to get messy.

SWEETS

Maybe you're one of those parents who think a child won't develop a taste for sweets if she never eats anything with sugar in it. This is your first baby, isn't it?

—Bill Dodds

Your baby has a natural sweet tooth that you can do little to suppress, but you can prevent it from getting out of hand.

Don't sweeten your baby's food with sugar or mix bland foods with sugary ones. Before you introduce fruits, make sure your baby likes vegetables. A cookie here and a piece of cake there are okay, but the majority of her snacks should be nutritious.

You probably can't give your child an aversion to sugar, but you can help her develop a preference for healthy food. In the years to come, other mothers will struggle with their children, begging and bribing them to eat healthy food. But you'll take comfort in the fact that your child chooses to eat healthy foods on her own.

Affirmation: I'll try to control my child's sweet tooth.

ACCEPTANCE

*Your responsibility as a parent is not as great as
you might imagine. You need not supply the
world with the next conqueror of disease or
major motion picture star.*

—*Fran Lebowitz*

Although you insist you simply want your child to
be healthy and happy (which of course you do!),
the truth is, you often wish for much more.

Sometimes you hope for amazing greatness.
What mother hasn't fantasized her child writing
the great American novel? Winning an Olympic
gold medal? Discovering the cure for cancer?

Other times you think you "see" potential in
your child from the day he was born. Mothers
constantly say, "Look at those fingers! When Josh
grows up, he's going to be a concert pianist!" or
"You can tell how smart Hannah is. She's going to
be a doctor or a lawyer!"

It's great to want your child to excel, as long as
you love your child exactly as he is. No matter
how your child turns out tomorrow and the next
day and the next, you need to completely accept
him today.

Affirmation: I'll accept my child exactly as he is.

SILLINESS

*Getting down on all fours and imitating a
rhinoceros stops babies from crying.*
—P. J. O'Rourke

Parents stop at nothing to entertain their
children—especially when it comes to turning
their children's sobs to smiles.

But even when your antics aren't needed to
distract or console, parenting includes regularly
making a fool of yourself. Inhibitions disappear
as you make moo-moo sounds, wiggle your ears,
and crawl on all fours just to get a laugh.

Consider yourself lucky. These are some of the
best moments of motherhood.

Affirmation: I'm willing to be silly.

AFFECTION

*Before the child ever gets to school it will have
received crucial, almost irrevocable sex education
and this will have been taught by the parents,
who are not aware of what they are doing.*
—Mary S. Calderone

You used to cuddle on the couch during the
evening news, steal kisses while doing the dishes,
and tenderly embrace when you came home from
work. But now that you're parents, you and your
partner may feel as if you're no longer free to be
affectionate anywhere but behind your closed
bedroom door.

Having a child shouldn't hinder you from
showing affection; in fact, it should encourage
you. Your child will learn about love, affection,
and romance from your example. If you save your
affection for behind closed doors, your child may
have a hard time expressing her own love.

And whether she understands it now, seeing
Mom and Dad show love for each other helps
your baby feel loved and secure.

**Affirmation: It's important for us to be
affectionate in front of our child.**

PROBLEMS

No one can say of his house, "There is no trouble here."

—*Asian proverb*

As you embark on your journey as a family, you hope and pray that you'll be the exception to the rule, that you'll magically escape the trauma of illness, financial woes, divorce, and all the other troubles that threaten a family's happiness and security.

But no matter how vigilant you are, your family will inevitably face hard times, times when you say to yourself, "This can't be happening to us."

The truth is, troubles will come, and you can't control them. What you *can* control is how your family will meet the challenges.

Your family can successfully weather hard times if each member feels free to express pain, fear, and disappointment. If feelings are shared rather than bottled up, you'll be able to support one another when trouble strikes.

Beginning today, make a commitment to encourage your family to be open and honest. It'll help you in good times or bad.

Affirmation: I can't prevent hard times, but I can help my family weather them.

A DAY IN THE LIFE

You want the grandparents to take care of your baby, but they do lots of things that make you uncomfortable, like spoiling him with treats. How can you express your concerns without starting a fight?

Regardless of how good your relationship is with your parents or in-laws, they inevitably do things with your child that make you wince. It's especially frustrating if you think they're repeating the same mistakes they made with you or your partner.

You have the right and obligation to protect your child, but assume that grandparents have only the best intentions. Be assertive—but not aggressive—when expressing how you'd prefer them to care for your child.

Remember, it's important to choose your battles. Chances are, if your baby gets a few extra treats once in a while, he'll come home none the worse for wear. If it's something critical, however, find the courage to resolve the problem.

Affirmation: I'm willing to give grandparents the benefit of the doubt.

COMPASSION

Having family responsibilities and concerns just has to make you a more understanding person.
　　　　　　　　　　　—Sandra Day O'Conner

Parenting has a deeply humanizing effect. You become kinder, more empathetic, more compassionate. You learn to set your own needs aside and put another person's first. More than ever before, you feel the pain, joy, frustration, and happiness of others.

That isn't to say that parenting is the only way to "grow a heart," but it's a darn good way. As you tuck your child safely into her crib, you say a prayer for her safety and well-being and for the safety and well-being of all the world.

Affirmation: Being a mother makes me more compassionate.

A DAY IN THE LIFE

Your six-month-old son wakes up several times at night and sobs uncontrollably until you comfort him. Should you comfort him each night or just let him cry and cry and cry?

This situation is difficult for mothers. If you let your child cry, you feel guilty and upset. How can you justify ignoring your child when he needs you? But if you rush to his side every time he cries, you worry he'll never learn how to comfort himself at night.

How you deal with this issue is up to you, but here's one solution that requires only persistence, an egg timer, and common sense: Decide how long it's okay for your child to cry and how long *you* can stand it without bursting into tears yourself. You might start with thirty minutes or perhaps only five.

Give it a week. Stick to your guns. Whenever you're tempted to give in, repeat to yourself: "I'm helping my child learn how to go to sleep."

Affirmation: I can teach my child good sleeping habits.

CONFIDENCE

A Girlfriend never lets ANYONE'S baby walk around in a terribly soiled diaper or with a runny nose if she has the tools to remedy the situation.
—*Vicki Iovine*

When you were a kid, not only would your mom spit on a tissue and use it to clean your face, but so would your friends' moms, your aunts, your grandmas, and the moms next door. These memories come rushing back the first time you clean your friend's baby's face or change your niece's diaper without being asked to do so.

Being a mother gives you the urge to keep your baby safe, clean, dry, and happy. Once you're confident in your mothering abilities, you feel compelled to offer the same services to any baby you come in contact with.

It's actually a wonderful feeling when you find yourself caring for some other baby, because just a few months ago, you barely had enough confidence to care for your own baby.

Affirmation: When I look after other babies, I'll know I'm confident being a mom.

FIRST WORD

In my book, "ma" and "da" do not count as a first word.

—Julian Orenstein

By now, your baby has made many noises that sound like words but really aren't. He's merely stringing sounds together, learning to form vowels and consonants in different combinations.

"Da" and "ma" are some of the first sounds babies make. This may explain why many people claim that *Dada* or *Mama* is their baby's first word, which often leads to undue boasting from one parent and undue disappointment from the other.

You may decide *Dada* or *Mama* is a bona fide first word, but you may also want to wait to rejoice until you hear a real word, such as *cookie*, *ball*, or *juice*.

Affirmation: I'll carefully listen for my baby's first word—no matter what it is or when it happens.

MARTYRDOM

A mother is a person, seeing there are only four pieces of pie for five people, promptly announces she never did care for pie.

—Tenneva Jordan

All too often, motherhood turns into martyrdom.

Although sacrifice is admirable, there needs to be a balance. If you never forgo your own pleasure to further your family's, you're selfish. But if you always sacrifice your needs and desires, you end up resentful, angry, and taken advantage of.

Beginning today, strive for a balance. Your child will grow up admiring your generosity and selflessness. But she'll also learn to respect you when you take care of your own needs.

Affirmation: I don't have to be a martyr.

"DIFFICULT" CHILDREN

Likely as not, the child you can do the least with
will do the most to make you proud.
                                    —Mignon McLaughlin

In recent years, a slew of books on raising
"difficult" children have hit the bookstores.

There are kids with serious behavior disorders
that clearly require professional attention. But
there are lots of children who are simply strong,
willful, precocious, and demanding individuals.

You know if you have one. Your baby sleeps
restlessly, isn't docile, requires lots of attention,
and is constantly on the go.

Having this kind of baby makes parenting
harder. It tests patience and requires ingenuity.
But it doesn't mean there's anything wrong—you
simply have a more willful child.

Affirmation: My child isn't difficult; he's strong.

PUSHING

*Pam and Edie are already giving Ivan violin
lessons and they're signing him up for a Tiny Tot
Transformation Seminar.*

—Jane Wagner

Years ago, I met a woman in a parent-child group
whose four-year-old son was an alum of the
Better Baby Institute.

Frankly, he didn't seem any better off than the
rest of the children in the class; if anything, he
appeared pressured and anxious, especially when
he was expected to perform.

Why must parents push their children? So the
children can develop their talents and potential?
So they can make their parents proud?

It's natural to want your child to achieve, to
keep up with the rest of the kids on the block.
But it's best to let him grow and blossom at his
own pace.

Affirmation: I don't need to pressure my child.

JOY

*Say the word "daughter" slowly…notice the way
it lingers on the tongue like a piece of candy.*
—Paul Engle

Right now, this very moment, close your eyes
and think about your baby. Take a break from
washing undershirts, changing diapers, or making
dinner, to savor all your pleasure in becoming a
mother. Caress your baby's perfect skin, feel the
sensual delight of cradling your baby in your arms,
recall the moment of birth and all the tenderness
filling you.

Now, slowly, say to yourself, "This is my son"
or "This is my daughter." Notice how the words
fill you with pride. And pleasure. And joy.

Affirmation: This is my child.

REJECTION

To find oneself jilted is a blow to one's pride.
One must do one's best to forget it and if one
doesn't succeed, at least one must pretend to.
                                                    —Molière

You can easily console the sitter and your friends when the baby rejects them. It's a bit harder to console yourself when she rejects you, reaching instead for your partner. When your baby rejects you, your initial reaction may be despair and confusion. You worry that she doesn't love you anymore.

Of course your baby loves you. Right now, she just needs something only your partner can give. You and your partner have different personalities and parenting styles. Perhaps one of you is tender; the other is lively. Sometimes your baby prefers your partner's style to yours.

Next time your baby turns away from you, take a deep breath, take a step back, and take stock of the situation. Determine what your baby needs and how you and your partner can best meet those needs. (And take comfort: Your baby will reach for you soon!)

Affirmation: Sometimes our baby prefers Mommy, sometimes Daddy.

EXHAUSTION

No animal is so inexhaustible as an excited infant.
—Amy Leslie

Many years ago, a study was conducted in which ten Olympic athletes spent an entire day following a baby, doing exactly as he did. Not one of the athletes could keep up. At the end of the day, they were flat on their faces, exhausted and panting, desperate for relief.

Whether your baby is six weeks, six months, or a year old, he's probably running you ragged. The relentless care of a newborn, the constant surveillance to ensure an infant doesn't swallow a penny or a baby doesn't scramble out of sight, is demanding work. If you're tired, it's no wonder!

When your baby's resting, rest. It's a matter of survival. If you're really feeling strung out, take a break. Hire a baby sitter, ask a friend or grandparent to help out, and do whatever you need to catch your breath.

Affirmation: Caring for a baby is exhausting!

GROWING UP

It will be gone before you know it. The fingerprints on the wall appear higher and higher. Then suddenly they disappear.

—Dorothy Evslin

When my children were tiny, I remember everyone saying, "The time goes so fast. Before you turn around, they're all grown."

Keep a record of all of it. Create scrapbooks and videos. Measure your child's growth with a chart on the bedroom wall. There's nothing silly about leaving a loaded camcorder or camera somewhere accessible in the house or about keeping a daily or even hourly journal in which milestones can be recorded. When you're out, ask your day-care provider or sitter to record any significant passages that happen in your absence.

Most of all, notice everything: the expressions on your child's face, what she says and feels, and how *you* feel as you watch the fingerprints on the wall get higher and higher and then suddenly fade away.

Affirmation: I'll notice every moment.

DISCOVERIES

No one shows a child the sky.

—African proverb

I find this proverb most reassuring. It reminds me that no matter how awesome the responsibilities of parenthood are, and no matter how much a mother must teach her child, there are some very important things children will learn on their own.

I remember watching Zoe, at six months, open and close a cupboard door, over and over, dozens of times, mesmerized by her discovery. Her amazement made me think of how Helen Keller must have felt when she first finger-spelled *water,* making the connection between the word and the water running over her hand.

There are countless opportunities to witness your child's learning: when your baby makes the connection between hunger and your breast, when he figures out how to back down the steps, when he realizes that the baby in the mirror is himself. Again and again, you're awed by your baby's joy of discovery.

Affirmation: What great discoveries my child is making!

PLAYPENS

…[T]he caged bird
sings of freedom.

—Maya Angelou

A playpen is a wonderful device when you need a moment of freedom, but keeping your baby in it too long infringes on her freedom.

Babies need freedom to explore their environment. It's vital to their physical, intellectual, and emotional development, especially after they're six months old. Fifteen minutes in a playpen while you take a break won't stunt her development, but keeping her in one for extended periods throughout the day may.

Even if your baby seems content in a playpen and even if she cries when you take her out, playpens should be used sparingly. Help your baby discover the world outside the playpen and the freedom it offers.

Affirmation: I'll use a playpen sparingly.

FLEXIBILITY

If there's a pitch you keep swinging at and keep missing, stop swinging at it.

—*Yogi Berra*

Perhaps you're determined to nurse until your baby weans himself, but hurrying home at lunch and having a breast pump at work is running you ragged. Perhaps you're dead set against imposing schedules, but the baby is up and down every fifteen minutes.

In other words, you're striking out!

Here's some coaching from World Series Champion Mothers: Give yourself a break. Your commitments are admirable as long as they up your "batting average." When they cause you to go down on strikes, it's time to rethink your approach.

Affirmation: I won't keep striking out.

FAITH

My children have a Higher Power and it's not me.
—Carolyn White

Thank God—or whoever or whatever your child's Higher Power may be!

It's a great relief to remember that there's a limit to how much you influence your child's life. Although you have mighty powers to create, protect, nurture, and guide, you don't have ultimate control over her destiny. Just as your life is subject to forces you can't always understand, so is your child's.

It is your task to guide your child on her spiritual path. Beyond that, you can only pray for her happiness and safety.

Affirmation: My child's on a spiritual path of her own.

IDEALIZATION

*Lovers, children, heroes, none of them do
we fantasize as extravagantly as we fantasize
our parents.*

—Francine du Plessix Gray

Parents are larger than life. To your baby, you're some sort of superhero, capable of bionic feats and achievements that keep him alive and happy.

As your child ages, he'll continue to idealize you. At one of my book signings, Evan asked if I were as famous as Michael Jackson. My own parents say that for years I imagined that we were much wealthier than we were. I distinctly recall telling my third-grade friends that I lived in a small castle.

It's flattering to be idealized; but it has its downside. When your child figures out you're simply human and not a mythic being, he may be disillusioned. It's best to teach your child from day one that you're fallible. Display your shortcomings as readily as your virtues. Your child will be less dazzled, but less disappointed in the long run.

Affirmation: I'll let my child see that I'm human.

FAMILY JOKES

Family jokes, though rightly cursed by strangers, are the bond that keeps most families intact.
—Stella Benson

The first time I shared Thanksgiving dinner with my husband's family, I felt utterly left out in the cold. It wasn't that they weren't friendly or warm or welcoming. It was the family jokes. I didn't get them. I didn't think they were funny. Gales of laughter over some shared memory of Thanksgiving past when his mother forgot to put the marshmallows on the sweet potatoes left me wondering if I'd married into a clan of lunatics.

Now that I'm a mother, I understand the importance of family jokes. Humor is a way of bridging generations and securing family ties.

Make a point to remember the funny little things that happen as you raise your child and become a family. Tell and retell these stories to your child—especially if she's the star. Years from now when your child proudly tells the tale of the "falling-down diaper," your shared laughter will prove how deeply bonded your family really is.

Affirmation: Family jokes help us bond.

DEPENDENCE

Children are dependent and needy by nature, not by choice.

—John Bradshaw

At times, you resent how much your child needs you. You feel burdened by his absolute dependence, his constant need for attention and care. When you feel this way, it's important to remember that although your child's dependence is a burden, it's a burden of love.

Next time you feel burdened by your child's dependence, remember that your child is physically and psychologically incapable of caring for himself. That doesn't mean you can't get angry and frustrated occasionally, but knowing he can't help being needy puts things in perspective.

When the burden feels especially heavy, also remember that every day you care for your child, you help him become more and more capable of caring for himself.

Affirmation: My child is dependent by nature.

DISCIPLINE

*Though the word "discipline" is associated
with structure, rules, and punishment in many
minds, it actually comes from the Latin word
for "teaching."*
—*Arlene Eisenberg, Heidi E. Murkoff,
and Sandee E. Hathaway*

The time has finally come. Your baby throws her
cup off the highchair, puts toys in the VCR, and
scatters the contents of the diaper bag across the
living room.

It's time for discipline.

But how much? How often? What best teaches
a baby values, morals, and acceptable behavior?

Saying no firmly yet gently can be effective, as
long as you don't overdo it. Removing the baby
from the trouble, distracting the baby, and
offering alternatives are also useful tactics.

However you decide to discipline, remember
to see yourself as a teacher, guiding your baby
as she learns self-control and right from wrong.

Affirmation: I'll use discipline to teach my baby.

BUSYNESS

Having children doesn't turn us into parents. It just makes us busy.

—Polly Berrien Berends

Remember your fantasies of motherhood? Rocking your baby in your arms, walking with the stroller in the park, reading fairy tales, playing Pat-a-Cake with those tiny little hands and perfect fingers.

Now you know the harsh truth. Parenting is often more about chaos than coziness. Sometimes entire days, if not weeks, go by when you feel as if parenting is merely about maintenance rather than meaningful connection.

Yet in spite of—or perhaps because of—all the clatter and clutter, you do become a mother. It happens along the way. The hugs and kisses you give as you're changing diapers, the giggles you share during bath time, the silly faces you make as you spoon-feed the baby a jar of strained carrots—these moments make you a mother.

Affirmation: I'll find the special moments in the mayhem.

FEAR

Perfect love casts out fear.

—1 John 4:18

Parental love is the most perfect love there is. Your capacity for affection, devotion, and protectiveness toward your child reaches far beyond what you've felt in any other relationship you've ever had or ever will.

Your fear is directly proportionate to your love. Whenever you open your heart, you risk having it broken. Your love for your child makes you vulnerable to pain and loss. Your love for your child makes the idea of anything happening to him unthinkable—beyond your worst nightmare.

How do you overcome such overwhelming fear? The answer lies in your love. Perfect love is unconditional—you love your child no matter what, standing by him in moments of darkness. Perfect love is trusting—you count on his resilience and trust your own ability to help him when he's in need. And perfect love is powerful— you have the strength, faith, and courage to love your child in the face of your fear.

Affirmation: My love is greater than my fear.

HISTORY

Our ancestors dwell in the attics of our brains as they do in the spiraling chains of knowledge hidden in every cell of our bodies.
—Shirley Abbott

Consider the power and mystique your ancestors hold over you. You've heard stories about those who came over from the old country on a boat, those who ran five-and-dimes during the Great Depression, or those who raised eleven children on a farm without electricity or running water.

Someday you'll be a framed photograph on your child's mantel, the stuff of family folklore, the subject of stories she passes on to your grandchildren.

Your child is your descendant. You are her ancestor. Together, you are history in the making.

Affirmation: I'm starting a new chapter in our family history.

A DAY IN THE LIFE

You and your mate have finally gotten it together to go out for dinner with the baby. An acquaintance whom you haven't seen in a while stops by and says to you, "How's the baby?" Then he turns to your partner and asks, "How's your job?" Why do you feel like throwing the platter of rigatoni in his face?

Because you're mad—and for good reason. Your friend's seemingly innocent yet obviously sexist comment diminishes both you and your partner and fails to acknowledge how each of your lives has changed as a result of parenthood. For all he knows, you have a full-time job outside the home and your partner is a stay-at-home dad.

Here's how you can educate your friend. Simply smile and say, "Our baby's fine. We're both very busy these days. Thanks for asking."

Affirmation: Parenthood has changed both of our lives.

COMPETITION

At play group, you mention that your baby sleeps through the night. Another mother counters that her baby does, too—only he did it sooner. You say that your baby's diapers once leaked onto your floor. The other mother says her baby's diaper leaked onto her neighbor's floor. It seems like you just can't win!

Who said parenting is a competitive sport? Do you expect some sort of prize for having the best baby or even for having the grossest stories?

When you're with other parents, you'll swap anecdotes about your adventures in parenthood. It's fun to hear how your lives are different yet the same.

But if you feel as if you can't contribute to the conversation without resorting to one-upmanship, perhaps you need to sit back and just listen. The purpose of the conversation is not to establish a winner or loser. It's to bond with other parents and realize that you're not alone in this endeavor.

Affirmation: I don't need to compete with other parents.

PROTECTIVENESS

If I seem to hold you too close and too tight, it is because I love you so.

—*Becky Daniel*

As a mother, you know your child needs to explore the world and gain independence, but sometimes you wish you could lock her in her room until she's twenty, hoping to keep her out of harm's way.

All mothers walk a fine line between healthy and obsessive protectiveness. While there's no way to eliminate your worry altogether, there are ways to keep your overprotectiveness in check: don't let your imagination run away from you and have faith in your child's resilience.

Affirmation: I'll keep my overprotectiveness in check.

DISCIPLINE

Children need love, especially when they do not deserve it.

—Harold S. Hulbert

Sometimes when your child misbehaves, it makes you angry. You want to yell at him, or give him the silent treatment. But be careful: Angry words or stony silence will give your child the message that you disapprove of *him*, not his actions.

Look at your child's face when he misbehaves. He already feels terrible; his face is crumpled up in shame and fear. Your child knows he has crossed the line, so you must be especially loving.

When you gently but firmly reprimand your child, then fold him into your arms for hugs and kisses, you give this important message: "I care enough to discipline you, and I love you even when you misbehave."

Affirmation: I'll discipline lovingly.

DIAPERS

I just figured out why changing diapers is such a pain. It's not the mess or the smell or the time involved that bothers me the most. It's the ungratefulness!

—Sandra Drescher-Lehman

Do you realize just what it means to change a diaper? Do you know how much sacrifice and selflessness it involves?

Of course you do, but it doesn't seem as if your baby does. You most likely don't hear a word of thanks. No, all you get is squirming and wriggling and fussing and crying. The only hint of gratitude you've noticed is those rare occasions when your baby refrained from soaking you or the changing pad.

It'd be easier to change diapers if you got some sort of thanks, but you'd still do it either way. You change diapers because your baby can't do it herself and because her health and happiness depends on it. You do it because you love your baby.

Affirmation: Changing diapers is a thankless task, but I do it anyway because I love my baby.

PARTNER

We know how powerful our mother was when we were little, but is our wife that powerful to us now? Must we relive our great deed of escape from Mama with every other woman in our life?
—Frank Pittman

When you control the details of your baby's life twenty-four hours a day, it's hard not to do the same with your partner's life.

The distinction should be obvious: your baby is a *baby*, but your partner is an *adult*. Your baby needs your supervision to survive. Your partner doesn't need your supervision, thank you very much, and he most likely resents it.

The responsibilities of motherhood are so great that mothers often feel as if they need to commandeer the entire family. Beginning today, realize that your motherly duties don't include "mothering" your partner. He's your equal, not your child. Plus, if he needs mothering, he'll go see his own mother—which may be another issue in itself!

Affirmation: I won't mother my partner.

EXTENDED FAMILY

*Within our family there was no such thing as a
person who did not matter.*

—Shirley Abbott

It's important for your child to appreciate the
deep connection he has with you and your
partner. At the same time, it's important for your
baby to know the special connection he has to
the extended family.

If you live near your baby's grandparents,
great-grandparents, aunts, uncles, cousins, and
other relatives, don't hesitate to introduce your
baby to them. Bring your baby to weddings,
reunions, summer picnics—any function that
gathers your family or your partner's family
together. For relatives who live far away, show
photos to your baby and tell him stories about
each person.

Being connected to an extended family widens
your baby's circle of love. And the wider the circle,
the more confidence he'll have when it's time to
venture out into the world.

**Affirmation: It's important for my baby to be a
part of an extended family.**

CONSISTENCY

*Like the rising and the setting of the sun each
day, be a constant for Baby.*

—*Becky Daniel*

There's a certain comfort in knowing that the
sun will rise every morning and set every night—
no matter what happens in between. It gives
definition and consistency to life, which can often
be unpredictable and chaotic.

It's very important to provide that same level
of consistency to your baby's life. She may feel
insecure, facing a barrage of new experiences
every day and not knowing what to expect next.

Like the sun, you can be the constant force in
your baby's life. She'll learn to count on your care,
love, and protection at all times. Your consistency
will give her the security and confidence to face
the surprises in life.

**Affirmation: Like the sun, I'll be a constant for
my baby.**

WORK

Work and love—these are the basics; waking life is a dream controlled.

—George Santayana

Being a new mother is overwhelming and stressful. At times you feel as if it's too much to handle, that there's too much to do and not enough time and energy to do it.

When your waking life seems to weigh you down, remember that a mother's life can be simplified into two parts: work and love. You work hard to nourish, teach, and protect your baby. You love your baby with powerful devotion and passion.

If you reflect upon your days and know that you've worked and loved, you can be confident that you've done all that life expects of you.

Affirmation: A mother's life is work and love.

LIFE

Many billions of years will elapse before the smallest, youngest stars complete their nuclear burning and shrink into white dwarfs. But with slow, agonizing finality, perpetual night will surely fall.

—Paul Davies

It's a somber, sobering thought. Even the stars so many light-years away, so full of energy and radiance, will dim and die.

As you gaze upon your baby, you're reminded of creation and life. Death is unimaginable and disturbing. But just as the stars cannot escape death, neither can you, your baby, or any living thing.

Don't let the inevitability of death keep you from living life to its fullest. On the contrary, understand that death is simply a part of life, and that every day of life is a sacred gift to be celebrated, shared, and appreciated.

Affirmation: Death is inevitable, but life is a gift.

APPRECIATION

*My daughters are lively, stimulating companions
who know that I enjoy their company.*
—Ellen A. Rosen

Does your child know you enjoy his company?
He probably knows it if you smile whenever
you're around him, if your body relaxes when he's
in your arms, or if you spend your day singing and
talking sweetly to him.

But your baby may be unsure if you pay little
attention to him or if you're always frowning,
distracted, and tense when he's around.

Your expressions, actions, and emotions let
your baby know if you enjoy his company. If your
baby feels as if he's your greatest companion,
then he'll feel loved, comfortable, and secure.
He'll know that you care for him not just because
you have to, but because you want to.

**Affirmation: I'll let my baby know that I enjoy
his company.**

MOTHER NATURE

I had never before seen the true image of
  the Earth
The Earth looks like a woman with a child
  in her arms.

                              —*Gabriella Mistral*

It's no wonder that the earth is personified as Mother Nature, a force who is as tender as she is powerful. Mother Nature brings forth life, and her creations inspire awe and respect.

   You are Mother Nature. Use this metaphor to empower your own life. You create life. You are an awesome force worthy of respect.

   Let this knowledge lift your spirits when you feel unappreciated and overwhelmed.

Affirmation: I am Mother Nature.

FOOD

So, I didn't bake cookies. You can buy cookies, but you can't buy love.

—Raquel Welch

For many people, images of motherly love are connected to memories of meat loaf, apple pie, and other culinary delights. Although my own mother worked full-time and hardly ever baked, I still recall with pleasure the one time I came home from school to the aroma of fresh gingerbread cooling on the counter.

You may feel like less of a mother if you use Hamburger Helper and instant mashed potatoes that are ready in just a minute and a half, or if most of your meals are takeout. You may feel as if your child will suffer unless you give her warm memories of homemade meals and treats.

Don't feel pressured. Your child doesn't care whether it's made from scratch or bought at a deli—as long as it's served with love.

Affirmation: I don't have to make meals from scratch.

ADOPTION

*Our innate desire and love for this little being
that has come to us, instead of through us, helped
to bring our child into a safe and loving world.*
                                    —*Beth Wilson Saavedra*

Motherhood is defined by love, devotion, compassion, sacrifice, bonding, and a great deal of hard work. It is not defined by genetics or the act of childbirth. Whether your baby comes to you or through you, you become a mother when you dedicate your life to caring for your child.

If you're an adoptive mother, know that biology doesn't create the bond you have with your child and the love that fills your heart, soul, and body.

You're a mother, and you're blessed.

Affirmation: Motherhood isn't defined by genetics.

REPLACEMENT

It's an old story—the oldest we have on our planet—the story of replacement.

—Sharon Olds

The birth of a new generation signals the passing of another. As Sharon Olds explains, it is a cycle of replacement. Your baby comes into the world as your grandparents, your parents, and even you begin to depart from it.

At Zoe's baby-naming ceremony, I was struck by the sad paradox of passing time. I was elated my daughter had arrived, but I also realized that I was no longer the baby of the family and that my grandmas were slipping away.

It's a sad fact, but a fact nonetheless. For now, be grateful for the gifts each generation can offer.

Affirmation: My baby's birth tells the story of replacement.

FAMILY VALUES

*[M]any people use…the phrase "family values"…
as a code word for exclusion.* This is what a family
looks like and if you don't fit the bill—if you're gay,
divorced, a single parent, a single person—too bad.
—*Judith Timson*

Family values is a buzzword used in many different contexts—especially in political rhetoric. When
some people advocate for "family values," they
mean that families should consist of a husband, a
wife, and approximately 2.3 children; they believe
so-called nontraditional families are dysfunctional.
Others lobby for family values because they
believe the family is one of the most important
institutions in our society and that it deserves
respect and political support.

In order to make sense of these varying
definitions, think about how you personally define
family values. But before you do that, think about
how you define family. Your definition of family
will no doubt influence your perspective on family
values and will help you understand which family-
values platform you want to support.

Affirmation: A family is _____
_____.

EMERGENCIES

Act quickly, think slowly.

—Greek proverb

When Zoe was around eight months old, she handed me a sheet of Sudafed tablets with two tablets missing. Within a nanosecond, I was in total panic mode, terrified she had swallowed the tablets.

I dialed poison control. As my heart raced, I could barely believe their directions: "See if the baby can punch out another tablet." She couldn't. That meant she hadn't punched out the missing tablets and swallowed them.

It was simple common sense, but I didn't have time to think it through when every second counted. All I could do was act quickly by calling for help.

To ensure you're ready to act when your child is in danger, keep emergency numbers by every phone, assemble a first-aid kit, and know infant CPR. You won't have time to think in an emergency; be prepared to act quickly.

Affirmation: When my child is in danger, I'll act quickly.

COMMUNITY

If you grow up where a snow mountain lifts its proud crown on the home horizon, in some strange way it becomes a member of your family.
—Margaret Craven

What makes your home horizon special? Do you see snowcapped mountains, a surging sea, towering skyscrapers? What about the cultural treasures that add flavor to your hometown? Is it known for cool jazz, mouthwatering fajitas, or historical architecture?

Don't let your child grow up taking these local treasures for granted. It's never too early to help your baby appreciate the beauty and uniqueness of his community. Take your baby to see the landmarks and sights, immerse him in the cultural experiences at an early age. Help him be proud of his home horizon.

Affirmation: I'll help my baby appreciate our home horizon.

MEMORIES

All grown-ups were once children, although few of them remember it.

—Antoine de Saint-Exupéry

Stop for a moment and recall your earliest childhood memories. You probably can't remember when you were as young as your child is now, but conjure up the world when you were a child.

Remember the crackling sounds of leaves beneath your feet, the sweet smell of your mother's perfume, fairy tales of faraway places as you drifted off to sleep. Remember, too, what scared you, what worried you, what you wanted to be reassured about.

It helps to recall these memories, especially at those moments when you're unsure of how to respond to your child.

It's good to remember that you, too, were a child once. Not so very long ago.

Affirmation: I remember that I, too, was a child.

SPECIAL NEEDS

*Others may look at her and see a severely
retarded, physically "crippled" child. I see my
beautiful daughter, bright and full of a special
love and hope. Someone once said to me,
"I don't know how you do it." I don't know
how I couldn't.*

—Hilde Schneider-Mott

If you're the parent of a child with special needs,
you're no doubt determined to help her lead a
healthy and happy life. To do that, you need
several things.

You need support from friends and family who will
offer hands-on help and provide sympathetic ears.

You also need to give yourself some latitude.
You worry about your child's happiness and
emotional health. You want her to succeed, yet
you know you can protect her only so much.

Finally, you need to know that she'll grow
strong only when you let her take on difficulties.
In her moments of mastery—and in her moments
of defeat—you learn what it really means to be a
parent.

Affirmation: Every child is special.

INTELLIGENCE

*Just because they happen to be a little shorter
than you doesn't mean they're dumber than you.*
          —Frank Zappa, with Peter Occhiogrosso

I wholeheartedly agree that children's short stature
has no bearing on their mental depth.

Children—even tiny babies—should be spoken
to respectfully. At first, it's best to use "parentese,"
a simplified form of language that helps your baby
learn to talk. But as your child develops, you can
use more complex language, knowing that he'll
quickly comprehend these new words.

Beginning today, commit to not talking down
to your child but to engaging him in intelligent
conversation (even if you're doing most of
the talking).

Affirmation: I'll respect my child's intelligence.

GRACIOUSNESS

Perhaps host and guest is really the happiest relation for [parent] and [child].

—*Evelyn Waugh*

How does a gracious host act? Warm, interested, sensitive, and eager to make guests feel comfortable and at home.

And how does a good guest act? Considerate, appreciative, and eager to lend a hand without being asked.

Not a bad model for parents and children. If you treat your child as a gracious host would treat a guest, your child will learn, in turn, to treat you as a good guest would treat a host.

Affirmation: I'm the host, and my child is the guest.

ACKNOWLEDGMENT

*There is no limit to the good a person can do, if
[she] does not care who gets the credit.*
                                        —*Paul S. McElroy*

Well, that puts an infinite limit on the good
mothers can do, seeing that they rarely get credit
for even a fraction of their deeds.

   Getting acknowledgment for all that you do is
not why you give, and it may not make your job
any easier, but it sure motivates you to be the
best parent you can. Because if you give and give
and give without any acknowledgment at all, after
a while you'll give reluctantly and resentfully
instead of gladly from your heart.

   There are two important, interrelated aspects
to acknowledgment: giving credit and taking
credit. Others will give you credit only if you take
credit—if you believe in the importance of what
you do. And the more credit others give you, the
easier it is to feel good about the innumerable
unspoken acts you're responsible for every
single day.

**Affirmation: To receive credit as a mother, I have
to take credit.**

OVERPROTECTIVENESS

Our child will not be raised in tissue paper! We don't even want her to hear the word princess.
—*Princess Juliana*

Even if you're raising a commoner rather than royalty, you struggle with how much you should protect your child.

Some parents opt for the "hard knocks" school of parenting. They expose their kids to the tough stuff as a way of preparing them for real life. Others choose the "tissue paper" school, coddling and controlling their children in an effort to keep them safe.

Neither strategy is successful in the long run. It's not healthy to willingly let your child experience pain and difficulties, just to "toughen her up." And it's also not healthy to smother your child, shielding her from the slightest hardship.

Your best bet is to give your child the freedom to explore the world, yet always be ready to guide her away from danger.

Affirmation: I'll won't coddle my child, nor will I expose her to pain.

LOVE

Do you have any idea how much I love you?
—All mothers

"I love you so much, if you measured my love it would be as big as the ocean. As big as the heavens. As big as a row of jelly beans lined up from one end of the earth to the other and then back again."

What mother hasn't said these words over and over to her child? And what child could possibly begin to comprehend the depth and breadth of a mother's love?

But even if your child doesn't understand the immensity of your love—even if you yourself don't understand it—it comforts him to hear you say it.

Affirmation: I'll tell my baby how much I love him.

PRAISE

Praise them a lot. They live on it like bread and butter.

—Lavina Christensen Fugal

Conventional wisdom once advised against praising children too much. Parents kept compliments to a minimum for fear of raising kids with swelled heads.

However well-meaning, that belief backfired in many cases. Many adults now struggle with low self-esteem. They would have grown up more confident—and become more effective parents themselves—if their parents had made as big a deal of their achievements as of their failings.

Today, parents are encouraged to lavish praise on their children. Praising your child does not give her a swelled head but instead strong self-esteem, which helps your child become a well-adjusted adult.

Starting today, you need to praise your child. Often.

Affirmation: Have I told my child today how wonderful she is?

SELF-FORGIVENESS

If you haven't forgiven yourself something, how can you forgive others?

—Dolores Huerta

Most people live with skeletons in their closets: stupid mistakes, haunting regrets, amends never made that weigh heavily on their hearts.

As a parent, it's especially imperative to forgive yourself for past mistakes. If you can't, it'll be hard to accept and forgive your child for the mistakes he'll make.

If you're compassionate with yourself today, you'll focus a less critical—and far more loving—eye on your child tomorrow. He'll come to understand that being fallible makes him no less lovable.

Affirmation: I forgive myself—and my child—for mistakes made.

APPRECIATION

Just the other morning I caught myself looking at my children for the pure pleasure of it.
—Phyllis Theroux

You spend hours staring at your child. You watch her worriedly, praying as she pulls up on the furniture and takes a tentative step. You scrutinize her, wishing her hair were curlier, her disposition were sweeter, that she'd get her first tooth like the other babies on the block have.

So how about just sitting back and enjoying the view? There's nothing more breathtaking than seeing your baby through unworried, uncritical, unconditionally loving eyes. Take a moment to look. Notice how fabulous your child really is. How beautiful. How amazing and unique. Gaze at your child for the pure pleasure of it.

Affirmation: Baby, I see you.

PARADOXES

*You begin to understand paradox: lying on the
bed next to him, you are deeply interested...and
yet at the same time you are deeply bored.*
                                        —Lydia Davis

Many paradoxes are present in motherhood. You
love being with your child, yet you can't wait for
the baby sitter to arrive. You wish time would stop
dead in its tracks, yet you anxiously wish your
child would grow up. Being with your child makes
you feel old and young, fearful and hopeful, rich
and poor—often in the very same instant.

There's nothing false about these paradoxes.
Both sides are true. Thankfully, the positives
exceed the negatives. Which is why, paradoxically,
you're able to spend hours staring at your child
while thinking about all the other things you have
to do.

**Affirmation: All of my feelings—however
paradoxical—are valid.**

INFANCY

I didn't have a baby in order to have a baby, I had a baby in order to have a child.

—*Carol Itter*

So many people feel this way!

If you're one of them, don't feel guilty and don't despair. There's nothing wrong if you prefer older kids. Lots of mothers adore cuddly newborns, while plenty of others adore kids who can carry on conversations and engage in lots of activities.

Both types of mothers are able to nurture their infants. And the good (or bad) news is, your infant will grow into a toddler, a preschooler, and eventually a teenager.

If it's a child you had in mind, just give it time. He's on the way.

Affirmation: All babies grow up.

AFFECTION

Don't be afraid to kiss your baby when you feel like it.

—*Benjamin Spock*

In fact, don't be afraid to kiss your baby even when you *don't* feel like it!

In most cases, there's no such thing as too much affection for a baby. Most moms lavish kisses and hugs on their children as spontaneous expressions of love.

Kisses go a long way. Sometimes they tickle, sometimes they soothe. Often they're better than words. Especially when your child is tiny, holding her closely and planting sweet, warm kisses on her forehead is one of many ways you say, "I adore you!"

Affirmation: I'll give plenty of kisses.

PRINCIPLES

Whenever two good people argue over principles, they are both right.
—Marie von Ebner-Eschenbach

You and your partner most likely have argued about a parenting issue, and if you haven't, you will. Some of these arguments are minor, such as whether to bathe the baby in the kitchen sink or the tub. Other arguments involve more serious parenting principles, such as whether to let the baby cry himself to sleep.

When you and your partner argue over principles, keep in mind you are both right. You both have the baby's best interest in mind, and you both want to be good parents. But you're two different people with different views, emotions, and experiences. There's no need to get defensive or accusatory with each other.

Knowing that neither of you is wrong will keep your arguments in perspective so you can focus on making the best decision for the baby.

Affirmation: We're both right when it comes to parenting principles.

ARSENIC HOUR

Between the nap and the twilight
When blood sugar starts to lower,
Comes a pause in the day's occupations.
That is known as the Arsenic Hour.

—*Anonymous*

It's the hour dreaded by most mothers. Dusk falls, exhaustion creeps up, your baby wakes up from her nap and screams for attention just as you're rushing to get dinner on the table. What can you do?

- Get help. Hire a neighborhood teenager to play with the baby from four to six, long enough to give you a little breathing room.
- Adjust naptime. There's no rule that says your baby must sleep from two to four. Try keeping her up a little longer and putting her down a little later.
- Nap when your baby naps. Instead of trying to get a million tasks done when your baby naps, rest yourself so you'll be refreshed and energetic in the late afternoon.
- Eat. Fruit or a high-protein snack—peanut butter or cheese and crackers—will help tide you over.

Affirmation: I can survive the Arsenic Hour.

MANNERS

*No matter how deep your love, you won't
enjoy his company much if he depends on
you for everything—and then doesn't bother
to say thanks.*

—Marguerite Kelly and Elia Parsons

It's never too early to teach your child to say
"thank you."

There are two ways to instruct your child in this
most basic social grace. First, encourage him to
say thank you whenever you help him or give him
anything. Second, remember to always say thank
you yourself.

Start now. When you hand your baby a
cracker, remind him to say thank you. He may
not understand the meaning of the words or
be able to repeat them quite yet, but sooner or
later he'll catch on. And when he hands you his
soggy cracker or brings you a book to read, be
sure you remember to say "Thank you!" with
great enthusiasm.

Affirmation: I'll teach my child to say thank you.

GROWTH

*[Children are] thrown into the works just to make
sure you're not getting too stagnant.*
—Susan Sarandon

Children are great at giving parents that proverbial
"kick in the pants."

During pregnancy, you redefine your goals and
values in anticipation of becoming a parent. Now
that the baby is here, you're learning how to
implement those goals and values in real-life
situations. Once your child begins to ask questions
of her own, you'll have to reexamine your beliefs,
asking yourself again and again who you are and
what you stand for.

What great insurance against stagnation!
By guiding your child in her journey, you, too,
grow and move forward. There's just no way to
stand still.

**Affirmation: Motherhood is a great opportunity
for growth.**

DESPERATION

"I'm getting divorced, selling the baby, running away," I inform Miriam.

—Phyllis Chesler

Of course she doesn't mean it. She's just had it, as most moms have felt from time to time.

The word to describe her feelings is *desperate*. Desperate for relief from the nonstop demands of motherhood. Desperate for a break from the overwhelming sense of responsibility. Desperate for someone—anyone—to take over for even a few minutes.

Divorce won't help. (You'd still have the baby, only with less support.) Selling your child isn't an option. (You'd never get enough.) But running away—to a friend's for tea or to the mall for an hour of window-shopping while the baby's with a sitter—can be exactly what's needed. It'll rejuvenate you just enough so you can look forward to mothering again.

Affirmation: When I'm feeling desperate, I'll take a break.

A DAY IN THE LIFE

You and your baby are enjoying story time with his favorite book. Rrrrip! Your baby now has half of the page in his hands. How do you respond?

That depends on whether your baby did it on purpose or by accident.

If your baby purposely ripped the page, you should firmly explain to him that pages are not to be ripped, that what he did was wrong. But those words will be unnecessarily harsh if your baby simply tried to turn the page and had a little trouble. Your baby will think it's wrong to turn pages. "Oops! Be careful!" is better suited if it were accidental.

As a parent, you need to learn how to tell a premeditated act from an unintentional one. It's not easy, and you'll probably make mistakes. But the important part is that you try your best to respond appropriately to each act.

Affirmation: I'll try to distinguish an intentional act from an unintentional act.

LAUGHTER

*Childhood is frequently a solemn business for
those inside it.*

—George F. Will

It's often tempting to burst out laughing at the
things your child does. Although laughter can
bring a family closer together, it's important to
know the distinction between laughing with your
child and laughing at your child.

When your child is smiling, giggling, and
obviously trying to entertain you, let yourself
laugh at her antics. But when your child seems
serious or sensitive, it's best to keep your
amusement in check, no matter how funny the
situation is.

A warm smile may lighten your child's mood,
but laughing out loud might hurt her feelings.
Always know that you can laugh all you want
once she's in bed.

**Affirmation: Even when it's funny, I'll be careful
to not laugh at my child.**

FEAR

It's like the smarter you are, the more things can scare you.

—*Katherine Paterson*

Your baby may have developed an inexplicable fear of sounds or objects that had never bothered him before. Suddenly, the movement of a battery-operated toy or the sound of the food processor reduces him to tears.

This is a sign that your baby's beginning to understand how the world operates. No longer a sleepy newborn, he's active and alert. As he explores the environment, he quickly realizes he's vulnerable to things that cause pain and confusion.

Your child must overcome these fears on his own, but you can facilitate the process. Without dismissing or compounding the fear, help your baby learn more about the object or sound. Don't force anything; go at a pace that's comfortable for your baby. Show him you're not afraid of it. This will help him build confidence and erase fear.

Affirmation: I'll help my child overcome fear.

HONESTY

The second time I lied to my baby, I told him he was the best baby in the world.

—Maxine Chernoff

This "lie" is so innocent and so common, it barely even belongs in the "white lie" category.

I "lie," too. I tell my kids all the time that they're the best, the smartest, the most wonderful children on the planet. It doesn't matter that most mothers say the very same thing to their children.

And why shouldn't you say your baby is the best baby in the whole wide world? Rest assured that no matter how far your child goes in life, regardless of how much success she achieves, no one will ever be quite so enchanted with her as you are.

Affirmation: I have the best baby in the whole world.

SELF-PRESERVATION

In the case of a crash, mothers of young children are advised to fasten their oxygen masks before fastening their children's…the same is necessary on terra firma.

—Joyce Maynard

No matter how often I fly, I'm always surprised by these instructions. I just can't imagine fastening my own oxygen mask while my child coughs and gasps and struggles for air during a sudden loss of cabin pressure.

But you can help your child breathe only if you're able to breathe yourself. By the same token, you can meet your child's needs only if you've attended to your own.

This may sound selfish. It may clash with your definition of a good (that is, selfless) mother. But you need to remember that in good times and in bad, you have to be healthy and whole in order to care for your child.

Affirmation: If I meet my own needs, I can meet my child's needs.

SKILLS

I know how to do anything—I'm a mom.

—Roseanne

As your child adds to his repertoire of skills, so do you. I asked several new moms to assess what they've learned so far. Here's a sample of what they said:

- Patience
- Flexibility
- How to do eight things at once
- Humor
- All the words to *Pat the Bunny*
- A dozen different things to do with flour, water, and food coloring

However, I suspect that Roseanne isn't referring only to all the things she now knows how to do; she's also referring to the increased self-confidence she gained through motherhood. As you rise to the challenges of motherhood, you discover how much you know and how much you have to give.

Affirmation: I've learned three new skills since having my baby:

1. _____.

2. _____.

3. _____.

HARD DAYS

After all, tomorrow is another day.
—*Margaret Mitchell*

All mothers have "those days." Your baby doesn't nap and instead crawls around the house, demolishing everything in her path like Sherman's army. Each minute is agonizingly slow—oh, will this day never end?

Take a deep breath. Tomorrow will come, and it'll be a better day. Tomorrow your beloved baby will surprise you by settling down for a three-hour nap or by cuddling up and enchanting you again with her sweetness and light.

Affirmation: Tomorrow will be a better day.

APPROVAL

*Don't say, "I love that picture." Say, "I can see
how high you stood on your tiptoes to paint that
yellow bird in the tree."*

—Connie Rubenstein

I was shocked when Connie, the child-development
expert who lectured our parent-toddler group,
made this distinction. Each time my two-year-old
drew a picture or picked up her toys, I'd exclaim,
"I'm so pleased by what you've done!" Apparently, I was missing the point.

When your baby stacks his blocks, don't say,
"I like what you did." That gives your child the
message that his success is based on your
approval. Instead say, "I can see how hard you
worked," or "I bet you feel great about what
you've done." Doing so helps your child find
satisfaction with himself for what he's done.

**Affirmation: I'll help my child develop a sense of
self-satisfaction.**

ORDINARINESS

Perfection consists not in doing extraordinary things well, but in doing ordinary things extraordinarily well.

—Angelique Arnauld

Every mother should post this quote somewhere highly visible in her home.

Sometimes it's hard to see the importance of the ordinary tasks you perform in a typical day as a mother. All you do is spend hours diapering, feeding, playing "How Big Is the Baby?" over and over with your child.

You used to do extraordinary things, important things. Maybe you trained for marathons, dazzled high-powered clients, organized the local library fundraiser, or played guitar in a folk band.

Someday you'll have time to do those things again, but you'll probably feel they aren't as important as they once were. You'll realize it's more important to be the best mother you can be, because those seemingly "ordinary" tasks make an extraordinary difference in your child's life.

Affirmation: I'm doing ordinary things extraordinarily well.

AWARENESS

I don't think my parents liked me. They put a live teddy bear in my crib.

—Woody Allen

Experts in child development generally agree that a child's psyche is most critically shaped between the ages of one and five. You have so much influence in such a brief period of time. What you do right now will affect your child for the rest of her life.

It's important to be conscious of the words you use, the way you touch, the choices you make, the lessons and experiences you give your child. But by the same token, it's important not to be overly vigilant, censoring your every word and action for fear that your child will end up hating you and spending a fortune on twenty years of psychotherapy.

The truth is, there's no way to avoid making some mistakes, no matter how psychologically savvy you are. What you can do, starting today, is be honest when you make a mistake and be aware of the messages you give your child.

Affirmation: I'll be aware of how I influence my child.

FIRSTBORNS

With the birth of our first child, we are initiated into motherhood.
—*Beth Wilson Saavedra*

Raising Zoe was harder than raising Evan. Zoe's every move, every decision, every tiny little cry was magnified. We consulted Dr. Spock constantly and called friends to report the first time she rolled over, the first word *(bath)*, the first step as if she were Neil Armstrong on the moon.

To be absolutely honest, I can't recall Evan's first word, and I turned around one day to discover him walking like a pro. We were more comfortable as parents by then. We simply trusted he'd grow up just fine without us fretting over every detail. As his father used to joke, "It's a wonder Evan learned anything, given how little we worried about it."

Raising your first—or only—child may be difficult. But not because your firstborn is a difficult child. Rather it's because being a first-time parent is harder than being a seasoned parent.

Affirmation: It's natural to worry a lot about the first child.

APPROVAL

The secret ingredient of fatherhood is approval.
—*Ellen Goodman*

Likewise, the secret—and perhaps most important—ingredient of motherhood is approval. Approving your child's decisions is a way of saying, "I love you even when I don't agree with you."

This is easier said than done. When your child plays with only the tattered, ugly teddy bear from the garage sale, and when your baby prefers to eat several small meals rather than three large ones, let your actions show your approval—don't force him to play with other toys or eat big meals.

Your child wants and needs your approval. It gives him the confidence to go out into the world knowing that his decisions are the right ones, even if you don't agree.

Affirmation: My actions will show my approval of my child.

TEENAGERS

You have a wonderful child. Then, when he's 13, gremlins carry him away and leave in his place a stranger who gives you not a moment's peace.
—Jill Eikenberry

Once your child becomes a teenager, you may believe in the gremlin theory.

It may be hard to imagine now. Your baby's just beginning to make noises that sound like words. How could she ever spend hours on the phone or, worse yet, mouth off at you? She's only beginning to notice other babies. How could she ever get caught up in dating and peer pressure? (And how could you ever deal with raging hormones, pimples, body changes, and "the talk"?)

Your baby will grow to be a teenager, and you'll be faced with a new set of parenting challenges. All you can do now is love your child and develop a bond that will last through the years—even when the gremlins show up.

Affirmation: My bond with my child will help me survive the teenage years.

GOSSIP

Don't gossip about the children of others while yours are still growing up.

—Jewish proverb

It's tempting to gossip, especially about children of neighbors or close friends. Sometimes it's a comfort and a relief to know that someone else's child struck a playmate or isn't walking yet. These juicy little bits of news may make you feel a little better about your own less-than-perfect child.

But gossip is damaging and dangerous. You risk spreading rumors that hurt others. Being superstitious, I prefer to censor my criticisms, knowing full well that someday my children may be whispered about behind closed doors.

It's safer and kinder to say only nice things and keep your judgments to yourself.

Affirmation: I'll resist the urge to gossip about other people's children.

BEDTIME

[W]e had broken together all the rules of bedtime, the night rules, rules I myself thought I had to observe…or become a "bad mother."
—Adrienne Rich

I remember when some friends remarked (rather smugly, I believe) that their kids were promptly put to bed at six-thirty each night.

As someone who struggled to get dinner served and cleaned up before eight, I was envious of the idea of a peaceful, child-free evening. But I was also a little concerned at the loss of what I considered one of the nicest parts of the day: being around the dinner table as a family, playing with the children as we all relax and catch up and enjoy ourselves.

What time you put your baby to bed is up to you, but consider what you're missing by putting him to bed too early. Also consider that the earlier you put your baby to bed, the earlier he'll wake up in the morning. (This idea probably won't sit well with you unless you put yourself to bed at six-thirty, too!)

Affirmation: I'll rethink the time I put my baby to bed.

A DAY IN THE LIFE

It's been a perfect day. The baby went down for two three-hour naps, and you did all the laundry, returned calls, and still had time to finish reading a novel. So what's so hard about being a mother?

Nothing, on a day like this, when everything goes right.

Every day has its own rhythm, its own challenges. Some days are impossible; everything that can go wrong does go wrong. Then there are idyllic days, when being a mother is everything wonderful you ever imagined and more.

The trick to surviving motherhood is to expect both ups and downs, hard days and easy days, times when parenting makes you wring your hands in frustration and times when you can't believe how lucky you are.

A perfect day gives you the perfect opportunity to stop for a moment, close your eyes, be thankful, and build the strength that will carry you through the not-so-perfect days.

Affirmation: I'm grateful for perfect days.

PEDIATRICIANS

*"There's nothing to worry about" is a typical
example of the kind of easy-for-you-to-say
remarks that pediatricians like to make.*
—Dave Barry

Contrary to popular belief, pediatricians don't say
"There's nothing to worry about" because they're
insensitive, too busy, or cavalier about your child's
health and well-being. In most cases, pediatricians
say it because, based on years of experience, they
truly believe there's no cause for concern.

Of course, it does nothing to alleviate a
mother's fears. In fact, it may make things worse.
You know your child best. If there were nothing
to worry about, you wouldn't be at the doctor's.
When your child is feverish or under the weather,
the last thing you want is to be dismissed with
such seemingly nonchalant reassurance. You want
your child's health taken seriously; you want every
inch examined, every symptom explored in full.

Only then will you be able to trust that there's
truly nothing to worry about.

**Affirmation: I'll trust my pediatrician, but not at
the expense of my own judgment.**

A DAY IN THE LIFE

After your child skips her nap, cries all the way to the grocery store, and then pushes two dozen cans of tuna off the shelf, you scream, "Stop it, or I'll never take you anywhere again!" Have you turned into Mommy Dearest?

Even the most patient and even-tempered parents get angry with their kids. It's human. Sometimes you lose your temper—no matter how much you love your child and no matter how sincerely you pledged to tread softly, speak quietly, and never, ever scream.

Next time you feel upset, try counting to ten or even one hundred. But if you still lose control and vent your anger, it helps to say, "I'm sorry I lost my temper. I'll try not to do it again," even if your child is too young to understand the words.

If you lose your temper a lot, it may be a sign that you need more support, a less hectic schedule, or possibly some counseling on dealing with anger. If you occasionally lose it, it simply means you're in good company with all the other imperfect parents trying to do their best.

Affirmation: Parents occasionally lose their temper. When I lose mine, I'll apologize.

POSITIVE REINFORCEMENT

Instead of punishing misbehavior, catch your baby being good.

> —Arlene Eisenberg, Heidi E. Murkoff,
> and Sandee E. Hathaway

Some days you feel like the only words you say to your baby are "No!" and "Stop!" and "Don't do that!" You know you need to teach him right from wrong, but such negativity wears thin on both you and your child.

As the old song says, you gotta accentuate the positive. Try this experiment: For one day, focus on positive reinforcement. Compliment your baby when he eats lunch without throwing half of it on the floor. Thank him when he brings you a picture book to read. Give him a hug when he lies still for a diaper change.

By the end of the day, you may feel a little better about the lessons you taught your baby. Positive reinforcement is often a better learning tool than punishment. That is, sometimes teaching what's right is more effective than teaching what's wrong.

Affirmation: I'll focus on what my baby's doing right.

LOVING

The giving of love is an education in itself.
                                    —*Eleanor Roosevelt*

On this point, all mothers should receive doctorates.

You know you're educating your child, yet do you recognize how much you, too, are learning in the process?

What do you learn from giving love? You learn to be generous of spirit—to tap deep inner sources of strength even when you feel tired and depleted.

You learn to be unconditionally accepting—to support your child even when you don't understand or agree with her. You learn to be unselfish—to put someone else's needs ahead of your own.

Above all else, you learn how loving you really are.

Affirmation: Motherhood is a constant lesson in love.

GIVING

You have not lived a perfect day...unless you have done something for someone who cannot repay you.

—*Ruth Smeltzer*

I guess this means any given day in a mother's life is pretty darn near perfect!

You give because you love your child, because it's up to you to make sure he's fed and clothed and nourished in every possible way.

There's no repayment. Your child can never give back what you've given him, just as you can never repay the love and generosity your own parents gave you. Children are not indebted to their parents; they don't need to justify their parents' love in any way.

Being a parent means giving out of pure love. Your reward is seeing your child become an adult who will pay it forward and give to others out of the goodness of his heart.

Affirmation: My child doesn't owe me a thing.

HOUSECLEANING

I'm going to clean this dump—just as soon as the kids are grown.

—Erma Bombeck

Face it. The mere presence of a baby can trash even the most beautifully kept home, turning it into a dump within minutes. Scattered toys, bottles and pacifiers, books and half-chewed Cheerios seem to proliferate before your eyes.

You feel bad for ignoring the baby while you try to keep a pristine home. But you also feel bad if you devote every moment to the baby and succumb to a messy home.

I recommend a compromise. First, let go of your prebaby notion of "home beautiful." Second, figure out how much time you can spend on housework and then tackle the areas that need the most attention.

Finally, don't feel guilty when you put the baby or the housework on hold at any given moment. Someday your house will return to normal—when the baby is grown. But for now, a compromise is in order.

Affirmation: I can balance the baby and the housework.

MENTORING

We have not sat at the feet of older women and learned from them.

—Barbara Jenkins

Long gone are the days of extended families where new mothers sat at the feet of elderly women and learned the mother wit, folklore, and secrets gathered over generations.

Today, most mothers collect parenting information from books, peers, and their mothers, but not from elderly women whose knowledge gained from a lifetime of experience could prove invaluable.

If your grandmother is alive, talk to her. Otherwise, seek out another elderly woman in your community. Find out what it was like for her to be a mother—the trials and triumphs, the mistakes, the lullabies, the herbal antidotes for sniffly noses. Even though some child-raising attitudes are outdated, the wisdom of elders can teach you how much of motherhood is timeless.

Affirmation: I'll learn from my elders.

TOYS

William wanted a doll.
He wanted to hug it
and cradle it in his arms...

—*Charlotte Zolotow*

When I was growing up, boys, unless they were "sissies," didn't play with dolls. They played with trucks and Lincoln Logs and squirt guns and toads, while girls spent endless hours dressing their Barbie dolls.

But times have changed. And thank goodness! Today's parents are no longer chained to gender-based traditions of the past. Parents now know how important it is to encourage boys and girls to make choices based on their desires, not on stereotypes that limit their creativity.

Boys should have dolls if they want them. Girls should crash trucks if they want to. They won't be harmed; they'll be happy and healthy.

Affirmation: I want my child to have every opportunity regardless of gender stereotypes.

GROUNDING

Children are the anchors of a mother's life.
—*Sophocles*

One day, a new mom came to me for counseling. She spoke of feeling overwhelmed, burnt out, about to lose it. Sometimes, she wearily confessed, she even contemplated running away and never coming back. "Of course I never would," she quickly told me, "because of my daughter. But if it weren't for her..."

As much as she exhausts, depletes, and overwhelms you, your child also grounds you. She gives you perspective when you're out of focus, she calms you when you're out of control, and she refocuses you when you forget what really matters in life.

And so you find the strength to continue because your child depends on you and you on her.

Affirmation: Motherhood grounds me.

CASUALNESS

*God knows that a mother needs fortitude and
courage and tolerance...[but] I praise casualness.*
                                    —*Phyllis McGinley*

Casualness! That's a trait rarely mentioned in
connection with motherhood, yet it's one of the
fundamental tools of the trade.

Witness, for example, a seasoned mother's
reaction to her eight-month-old baby toppling
from a kitchen stool. She calmly reaches to
retrieve him, and in her most even voice asks,
"Are you all right, honey?" while checking for
bruises and bumps. The baby takes his cue from
her and soon happily resumes playing.

Cultivating casualness has long-term benefits.
Today, the slightest arch of the eyebrow prevents
your baby from pushing buttons on the VCR.
Tomorrow, the understated "Aren't you a little
late?" when your teenager comes home after
curfew keeps panic under control and punishment
in perspective.

Here's the key: The less you overreact, the
more power your words and actions have when
you really need to make an impact.

Affirmation: I'll keep things casual.

FUSSING

Perhaps a child who is fussed over gets a feeling of destiny, he thinks he is in the world for something important.

—Benjamin Spock

Fussing doesn't mean spoiling; it's a way of making your child feel special, cherished, worthy of great and wonderful things.

And fussing doesn't necessarily mean making an overly big deal of your child. You fuss when you spend ten minutes lovingly brushing your child's hair, when you clap and laugh as you watch your child build and topple twelve consecutive block towers.

Every child should be fussed over as if she were the most terrific child in the world. Perhaps then we'd have a world filled with children who value themselves and know that they are loved.

Affirmation: My child deserves to be fussed over.

LOVE

Love is like a violin. The music may stop now and then, but the strings remain forever.
—June Masters Bacher

Okay. You admit it. Sometimes you don't like your child or even think he's cute. To be perfectly honest, sometimes you wish he belonged to someone else. Does this mean you don't love your baby?

If you're worried about feeling this way, stop. Even the most devoted mother has her moments—sometimes even hours and days—when she doesn't particularly like her baby.

It doesn't mean you've stopped loving your child. It doesn't mean you've failed as a mother. It means you must accept your feelings, trust that you love your child, and keep doing a good job.

Affirmation: I may not always like my child, but I'll always love him.

HANDS

The sweetest flowers in all the world—
A baby's hands.

—Algernon Charles Swinburne

Oh, those hands. Those fragile petals that wrap around your finger, sweeter than the sweetest rose.

A baby's hands are among the purest things on earth. Miracles of nature so dear, so innocent, they give you goose bumps.

Take a moment, right now if possible, away from your responsibilities, away from your everyday demands, and simply take your baby's hand in your own. Feel its velvety touch. Smell its fragrance. Stroke each tiny finger and hold it close to your cheek. Turn it over a few times and simply notice how amazingly perfect it is.

Affirmation: My baby's hands are beautiful.

A DAY IN THE LIFE

At your play group, you notice that the other moms are much sterner when it comes to discipline. One mother always uses a firm tone. Another mother skips words altogether and immediately scoops up her baby when he gets into trouble. Your baby responds when you say her name. Does this mean you're a better disciplinarian?

No, it simply means each baby has an individual personality and each mother has adapted a form of discipline that best suits her child.

If the other moms used the same discipline tactics you use, their babies would probably ignore them. Some babies are determined and willful; they won't respond unless they hear strong tones or are physically removed from trouble. Other babies are highly sensitive and will heed subtle disapproving tones or expressions.

Each mother needs to use disciplinary tactics that fit her child's personality. This doesn't mean one style is better or worse than another— just different.

Affirmation: I'll use discipline that suits my baby's personality.

JUGGLING

*Any mother could perform the jobs of several
air-traffic controllers with ease.*

—Lisa Alther

Have you ever witnessed a group of moms visiting
over coffee? It's an amazing scene! Phones ring,
toys fly, "owies" get Band-Aids, and sticky Jell-O
fingers get washed and washed again while the
mothers pick up threads of a conversation started
fifteen minutes earlier without skipping a beat.

Moms cultivate the ability to do a million
things at once out of necessity. It requires focus,
flexibility, and a sense of humor.

Moms can focus their attention on the
most compelling need of the moment, which
changes constantly.

Moms are flexible. They can quickly adapt their
expectations and plans.

Moms laugh and keep things in perspective,
always prepared for something new.

Affirmation: I can juggle many things at once.

A DAY IN THE LIFE

While visiting your neighbor, you suddenly hear the sound of shattering glass as your baby pushes a lovely vase off a coffee table. As your neighbor's face turns white, you wonder how you could have raised such a terrible child!

Your child isn't terrible, but it is awful when your child does something wrong. One of my worst parenting moments was when Evan, then three, smacked another child across the shoulders with a baseball bat. I've never forgotten the waves of humiliation as people stared, shaking their heads at the "bad child" and his "bad mother."

You take it personally when your child acts out, just as when he's well behaved. But you need to know that his behavior—good or bad—usually isn't a direct reflection of your parenting.

You're responsible for helping your child know right from wrong. You're not responsible for your child's mistakes. Sometimes he just blows it. You need to find appropriate consequences, forgive him, and forgive yourself.

Affirmation: I'm not responsible for my child's occasional outbursts.

PATIENCE

*Have patience with all things, but first of all
with yourself.*

—*Saint Francis de Sales*

It's easy to be frustrated with yourself when you're
cranky with your child, when you fail to anticipate
her needs, when you fall short of your expectations of what it means to be a good mother.

You can spend the next twenty years counting
and regretting your mistakes. Or you can learn to
be patient with yourself and accept that you have
good days and not-so-good days.

It isn't easy to be a parent; in fact, it's one
of the most complex challenges in the world.
Perfection isn't required. You needn't get it right
all or even most of the time. All that's required is
your best effort and the willingness to give
yourself plenty of slack.

Affirmation: I'll be patient with myself.

CHILD RAISING

Children should be seen and not heard.
—Anonymous

Many traditional child-raising beliefs are now being questioned: "Children should be seen and not heard," "A good child always does what his parents say," and "Father knows best."

Today, parents believe that children should be encouraged to express themselves, that compliance isn't always appropriate, and that fathers and mothers alike don't always know best.

It's important to ask yourself whether traditional parenting "words of wisdom" are truly wise, whether they actually contribute to your child's healthy development and positive self-esteem. Even though your baby is young, you need to decide for yourself what parenting beliefs best suit you and your child.

Affirmation: I'll form my own child-raising beliefs.

UNDERSTANDING

What children expect from grown-ups is not be "understood," but only to be loved....

—Carl Zucker

Don't try to understand some—or most—of your baby's actions. Don't bother figuring out why he likes having pudding on his toes. It's impossible to decipher what *ya-da-ga-ga-ba* means. You can't even pretend to comprehend why he screams bloody murder whenever you empty the Diaper Genie.

Your baby doesn't expect you to understand him. He may not even understand himself. In many cases, asking "why" is unnecessary. What is necessary is love. Your baby expects you to love him. That means he expects you to let him enjoy the pudding on his toes, babble up a storm, and empty the Diaper Genie while he's napping.

Affirmation: Understanding my baby isn't as important as loving him.

GARBAGE

I'm not your garbage can.

—*Anonymous mother*

Walking down the street in Berkeley, I overheard a woman say this to her six-year-old son after being handed a dripping ice-cream cone, three bottle caps, and a well-chewed wad of gum.

I laughed out loud, then agreed with her. Why do children assume that mothers are the designated receptacles of their junk? More importantly, why do mothers take it from them instead of insisting the children take care of it themselves?

At first it's cute when your baby hands you her half-eaten cracker. But if you don't take action, she'll be handing you all sorts of half-eaten and half-used junk until she's eighteen.

There's a way to nip this in the bud. The next time your child gives you a handful of soggy Cheerios or the crusts from a peanut butter sandwich, don't eat them and don't toss them. Make a game of having her throw them in the garbage can herself.

Affirmation: I'm not a garbage can.

TEARS

It is such a secret place, the land of tears.
—Antoine de Saint-Exupéry

When your child weeps, you automatically say, "Honey, don't cry."

Are you truly comforting him? Or are you giving him the message that tears are bad, that they should be hidden or wiped away? And do you let your child see your own tears? Or do you hide your sorrow and muffle your tears behind a cheery façade?

It hurts to see your child cry. But you hurt him more when you don't allow him to express pain and sadness freely. Likewise, if you don't express your own sadness, you teach your child to cover his, too.

So comfort your child, but let him know that he can cry and that you, too, sometimes cry. Tears will be less scary, less secretive. They'll simply be part of life.

Affirmation: Crying is a natural part of life.

ARGUING

We never quarreled in front of the children.
—Jehan Sadat

Although constant fighting between parents alarms and damages children, there's nothing wrong with an occasional disagreement. You and your partner most likely have differing opinions, and when you do, it's better to work them out than to put on a false united front for your child's sake.

In fact, it's healthy for your child to see you negotiate differences, as long as it's done in a respectful manner. Even when there's a bit of anger expressed, it's important for your child to grow up knowing that family members can argue without causing irreparable harm or losing one another's love.

Affirmation: Parents don't always have to agree.

INTUITION

Trust your hunches.

—*Joyce Brothers*

Jacob, Bonnie's six-week-old baby, just didn't seem right to her. Even though he wasn't running a temperature, she took him to the doctor. Sure enough, he had viral pneumonia.

There's just something about a mother's hunches. You know your child; you notice the subtle ways in which she's upset or worried or under the weather.

Trusting your intuition doesn't mean you ignore expert advice or always assume you're right. It just means that when it comes to your child, you take your own perceptions seriously and listen to your heart.

Affirmation: I'll trust my hunches.

LIMITS

Oh, and at least once a day say "No."
—Erma Bombeck

It's one of the most useful words in a mother's language—and one of the hardest.

But saying no is fundamental to your child's development; in fact, it's much more important than appeasing him at every turn. It's a loving way to say that you care enough to set limits and guidelines for your child to follow.

Today, you're saying no when your baby climbs onto the coffee table and when he doesn't share a toy with a playmate. It won't be long before you're saying no when your child wants to watch TV before his homework is finished or when he wants to stay out until midnight with friends.

Saying no won't win you popularity contests in the short run. But it ensures that your child will learn lessons that will help him in the long run.

Affirmation: Sometimes saying no is a way of saying "I love you."

MISTAKES

Telling lies and showing off to get attention are the mistakes I made that I don't want my kids to make.

—*Jane Fonda*

It takes courage to admit your errors. But it's impossible to guarantee that your child won't follow in your footsteps and make the same mistakes.

You can commit today to be a positive role model, but it won't ensure that your child will avoid repeating your mistakes. Your child has her own path to follow; the mistakes she'll make will be powerful, necessary life lessons, even if they're the exact same lessons you've learned over the years.

You can share what you've learned from your mistakes, point out the pitfalls. But you don't have the power to prevent your child from making mistakes.

Affirmation: I can't keep my child from making mistakes—even the same mistakes I made—but I can try.

A DAY IN THE LIFE

The ten-year-old next door is whiny, mean, and rude, but his mother does nothing to discipline him. In fact, she seems to encourage that behavior. She says she accepts her son's personality and to discipline him would be to reject him for who he is. Is this how you should raise your baby?

Your neighbor is right: Parents need to accept their children's personalities and love them for who they are. But you need to separate your child's personality from his behavior.

If your baby is stubborn, you shouldn't change that fundamental trait. After all, his stubbornness keeps him from giving up when learning to master a spoon gets difficult. But that doesn't mean you should encourage your baby to throw tantrums whenever he doesn't get his way. You need to teach him that such behavior is unacceptable.

Love your child for who he is, but love him enough to teach him positive, healthy ways to display his personality.

Affirmation: I'll accept my baby's personality and discipline his misbehavior.

LOVE

Nobody has ever measured, even poets, how much a heart can hold.

—*Zelda Fitzgerald*

How do you measure the overwhelming joy, gratitude, and passionate protectiveness your child inspires?

You measure it in the smiles that radiate at the sight of your child. You measure it in the tears that flow when you're flooded with tenderness for your child. You measure it in the pride that swells until you feel as if you'll burst with love for your child.

You measure it, and you realize that your heart can hold more than you ever imagined possible.

Affirmation: My love is boundless.

EXPENSES

*I could now afford all the things I never had as
a kid, if I didn't have kids.*

—Robert Orben

I've met lots of women in their late twenties,
thirties, and even forties who hesitate to take on
the financial burden of parenthood. "I've worked
so hard to make it," they say. "Why blow it all on
diapers, strollers, not to mention the cost of a
child's college education?"

Yet ask any mother, well-off or struggling, and
she'll undoubtedly say the benefits of having a
child greatly outweigh the costs. You may sacrifice
and deny yourself luxuries (and sometimes
necessities as well), yet what you're given in
return enriches your life beyond measure.

Affirmation: Motherhood is worth every penny.

GROCERY SHOPPING

I was doing the family grocery shopping accompanied by two children, an event I hope to see included in the Olympics in the near future.
—Anna Quindlen

Shopping with a child takes strategy, determination, and twice as much time as it took back when you had the luxury of shopping solo. Here are some tips:

- DO bring a list. Don't veer off course even if your child begs for Froot Loops and Gummi worms.
- DON'T shop anywhere where you have to bag your own groceries. You save money when you bag, but you lose sanity.
- DO bring a snack she can eat in the cart.
- DON'T plan to do much else that day; you'll be exhausted by the time you're finished.
- DO change her diaper before you go. It's not sure-fire, but it increases your odds of not having to abandon your cart in the middle of the produce section to find the restroom.

Affirmation: I deserve a medal for grocery shopping with a baby!

NAPS

*You learn never to count on anything being the
same from day to day, that he will fall asleep at a
certain hour, or sleep for a certain length of time.*
—Lydia Davis

Some mothers try to force strict naptime
schedules, not for their babies' benefit but for
their own. They put their babies down for a nap
at the same time each day whether the babies are
tired or eager to play.

Ironically, the more you try to control naptime—
manipulating schedules, wishing and hoping (and
praying) the baby will sleep on cue—the more
frustrated you get.

Your baby will sleep when he's ready, and not
a moment before.

Affirmation: I can't control my child's schedule.

INTELLIGENCE

Every child is born a genius.
                                        —*R. Buckminster Fuller*

Certainly, R. Buckminster Fuller didn't mean that every child comes into the world with a staggering IQ and the potential to win a Nobel Prize.

More likely, he speaks of the innate intelligence each child possesses, which, if neglected, can be dulled or even extinguished.

How do you keep the spark alive? Read to your child from the time she's born. Never talk down to her, even when your baby is unable to understand most of your message. Nurture her creativity. Commit to take an active role in her education.

And always—always—believe that your child is capable of greatness.

Affirmation: I'll nurture my child's innate intelligence.

A DAY IN THE LIFE

You're going up the escalator at the mall with your ten-month-old in tow when you notice another mom screaming at her dawdling toddler, "Get going or I'll never take you anywhere again!" You recoil as she grabs the back of his neck and smacks him on the behind. What's the right thing to do?

This is a wrenching ethical call. You want to speak up, but you're scared, and for good reason. What right have you to judge another parent? What if you end up in a screaming match with this stranger in the middle of a crowd?

You need to ask yourself this question: "Is there something I can do to help the child?" If the answer is yes, then be sure to intervene carefully and with compassion. If the answer is no, use this experience to give new perspective on how you yourself discipline your child.

Affirmation: All parents are responsible for the safety of children.

COMMUNITY

*One hesitates to bring a child into this world
without fixing it up a little.*

—*Alta*

As a parent, you have a responsibility to "fix up"
your community in whatever ways you can: by
organizing neighborhood crime protection, by
helping the homeless, by working to create a safer
and healthier environment.

When you do your part, you achieve two
important goals: You improve your quality of life,
and you show your child the importance of community service.

You don't have to change the world; you
simply have to do your small part for your
child's sake.

**Affirmation: I can make a difference in
my community.**

SAVINGS

Blessed are the young, for they shall inherit the national debt.

—Herbert Hoover

In the twenty-first century, it's easy to feel discouraged about your child's financial security. Will you be able to send him to college? Will he have the financial resources to buy a home someday? Will Social Security be obsolete by the time he's old enough to qualify—by the time *you're* old enough to qualify?

It's never too soon to start saving. Fill a piggy bank with pocket change, open a bank account in his name, ask for savings bonds rather than toys as gifts, and put money in an IRA or another long-term investment.

Anything you put away now will help your child bank on a secure financial future.

Affirmation: I'll save for my child's future.

SLOWING DOWN

*It can take practice for adults to change over
every so often to Children's Standard Time.*
— Fred Rogers and Barry Head

Mothers are always rushing, and children are
always dawdling.

It's easy to feel impatient when you're running
late and it takes fifteen minutes to get your baby
to stay still long enough to change a diaper, or
when she spends twenty minutes staring at (and
dissecting) a handful of dandelions while you
struggle to get her jacket on.

If there's truly no time to waste, then do
whatever it takes to stay on schedule, even if it
means hurrying your child along. But if there's no
rush, try to adjust to Children's Standard Time. It's
slower, dreamier, and a nice break from the fast
pace of adulthood.

**Affirmation: It's nice to slow down once in
a while.**

TANTRUMS

A mere parent pitted against a child in a test of wills in a toy store is a terrible spectacle.
—*George F. Will*

There's only one thing worse than a tantrum, and that's a tantrum in public.

Most parents experience this nightmare during the "terrible twos," but early forms of tantrums can happen in the first year. They usually occur in crowded places—the grocery checkout line, the middle of a department store, or during a church or synagogue service.

So what's a parent to do with a screaming, hysterical child who's flung himself on the floor?

First, stay calm. Laughing or getting angry will only encourage the behavior. Act as if you've barely noticed. In your most matter-of-fact tone, instruct your child to get up, or if you must, pick him up and remove him from the premises.

Second, remember this, too, shall pass. Unless your child has serious behavioral problems, most kids grow out of the tantrum stage by the time they're four or five.

Affirmation: Staying calm will help me get through my child's tantrums.

NUTRITION

We are allowing a majority of our children to form atrocious dietary habits.

—Benjamin Spock

You want to provide a healthy diet for your child. In early childhood, your child builds bones, grows teeth, and develops eating habits that will serve—or sabotage—her for the rest of her life.

Despite their best efforts, many mothers have days when they fall short of following nutritional guidelines in preparing their children's meals. Much as the food pyramid weighs heavily on their minds, sometimes peanut butter and jelly, microwave ravioli, or a delivery pizza are simply the best they can do.

While it's important to take your child's diet seriously and try to provide healthy meals every day, it's just as important not to pressure yourself if you can't always manage a protein accompanied by a fresh green vegetable. Fast food in moderation isn't atrocious, as long as you don't make a steady diet of it for your child.

Affirmation: I'll do my best to provide a healthy diet for my child.

DISCIPLINE

He who spares his rod hates his son.
—*Proverbs 13:24*

Although some parents believe spanking or hitting is an effective way to discipline, I'm not one of them.

While physical punishment certainly sends a strong message, you have to question exactly what that message is. When you hit your child, even in his "best interest," you teach two things: you are more powerful, and violence is acceptable.

All forms of discipline require a bit of "tough love," but physical punishment takes it to the extreme. With understanding, respect, and patience, you can discipline your child in more loving and effective ways.

Affirmation: I'll learn better ways to discipline my child.

LANGUAGE

When I was born, I was so surprised I couldn't talk for a year and a half.

—Gracie Allen

I once heard of a child who didn't speak a word for the first four years of his life. He was examined by numerous specialists, and no one could figure out what was amiss. When he was four and a half, his family moved to England. As the airplane landed, he turned to his mother and asked, "Where are we?" Apparently he hadn't needed verbal language until then.

There are children who talk clearly at nine months and others who babble until they're two. Every child is different. But when that first word (and the second and the third…) comes, it'll be music to your ears.

Affirmation: My child will speak when she's ready.

AUTHORITY

*No matter how much kids resent authority, they
resent even more being left with none at all.*
—*Art Linkletter*

Many parents resented their own parents'
authority. So they bend over backward, giving
their children unlimited freedom.

The irony is, the more you relax the rules with
your child, the more desperate he is for structure
and discipline. Your child wants and needs you to
be in charge. As one child put it, "Moms and dads
are s'posed to know what to do so they can tell
me what I'm s'posed to do."

Being in charge doesn't make you a dictator.
It simply gives your child rules and boundaries
so he won't be overwhelmed by a world much
too big and much too complex for him to figure
out alone.

**Affirmation: My authority makes my child
feel secure.**

DEPENDENCE

My obstetrician was so dumb that when I gave birth he forgot to cut the cord. For a year that kid followed me everywhere.

—Joan Rivers

When your child is little, it's almost as if she's attached to your hip. She follows you everywhere—hanging on your arm while you're trying to talk on the phone, nipping at your heels wherever you go, wanting to sit in your lap even when you go to the bathroom.

When you've simply got to have some space—because your arms are full of groceries, because there's someone at the door, or just because you need a brief respite—an infant swing or a playpen are helpful.

It's a drag to be pulled on constantly. But the good news is, your child will pull away gradually, until you're lucky if you can get her to stay in the same room with you for more than a few minutes at a time.

It may be hard to imagine now, but enjoy your child's company while you can. Pretty soon you might wish there weren't so much space between you.

Affirmation: I'll give myself a little space.

WEANING

Mothers can get weaned as well as babies.
—Thomas Chandler Haliburton

Whether you or your baby initiates the process, weaning is a challenging transition.

Some babies show a readiness for weaning before their mothers are ready. When babies suddenly reject the breast or seem uninterested in nursing, the mothers are devastated. Other mothers feel guilty about weaning when their babies aren't ready. They find it difficult to withhold something they once gave so freely to their babies—especially when the babies aren't ready to give it up.

As with all stages of motherhood, weaning requires patience, determination, and love. Though you need to say good-bye to this beautiful part of your relationship as mother and child, take comfort in the fact that weaning is a natural part of your baby's development and your growth as a parent.

Affirmation: Weaning is a bittersweet yet necessary stage for my baby and me.

MANNERS

Good manners have much to do with the emotions. To make them ring true, one must feel them, not merely exhibit them.

—Amy Vanderbilt

Like all parents, you hope your baby will someday say "please" and "thank you." Beyond that, you hope he'll someday wait patiently in line at the movie theater, pick up litter, and help senior citizens carry groceries out to their cars. In short, you want your child to be truly thoughtful and courteous, rather than begrudgingly polite because it's the "rule."

To ensure this, you need to instill in your child the importance of treating others with utmost respect and consideration. If your baby grows up caring deeply for others, good manners will surely follow.

Affirmation: I'll teach my baby that good manners come from the heart.

SELF-ACTUALIZATION

To be a really good, creative mother you have to be an extraordinary woman.

—Meryl Streep

Patience. Ingenuity. Creativity. A great capacity for love. These are few of the basic qualifications needed to be a mother.

But to be an extraordinary mother, you need to be more than a mother. You need to be a well-rounded woman, constantly developing your talents, honing your skills, deepening your spirituality, growing as your child grows.

Affirmation: I'm growing as a mother and as a woman.

RESISTANCE

*Cosby's First Law of Intergenerational Perversity:
No matter what you tell your child to do he will
always do the opposite.*

—Bill Cosby

Is this because children are innately contrary?
Do they automatically ignore parents' wishes in
order to aggravate them? Do they take perverse
pleasure in giving parents a hard time? In other
words, do they say no just because parents want
them to say yes?

Sometimes. When kids, even babies, are
resistant, it's their way of asserting independence
and expressing their own points of view.

When your child appears to be difficult just for
the sake of being difficult, it helps to remember
what little power she really has. Two strategies:
Give her as much say as possible about as many
things as you can, and avoid giving her more
power by overreacting to her resistance.

**Affirmation: My baby's resistance is a way to
assert independence.**

SICKNESS

When your child is sick, all perspective slides into the ocean.

—Liz Rosenberg

When mothers say to their sick children, "I wish it were me instead of you," they really mean it. There's nothing more miserable than sitting by helplessly as your child wheezes and coughs, moans with the stomach flu, or nurses a broken collarbone. You'd do anything—*anything*—to ease his pain.

Yet all you can do is attempt to comfort him by taking him to the pediatrician, giving him plenty of juice, reading him stories, and placing a cool hand on his fevered brow.

It's frightening when your child is sick. It reminds you of how fragile he is and makes you immensely grateful once he's back to his healthy, vigorous self.

Affirmation: I'd do anything to ease my child's pain.

NAKEDNESS

"I'm Ted. I'm 10 Months Old and I'm a Nudist."
—Julian Orenstein

Some babies love to be naked. You know this if your baby dashes away, squealing and giggling and baring it all, while in the middle of a diaper change or after bath time.

Try to see being naked from your baby's perspective. Diapers are bulky and cumbersome. Clothing is restricting. There's something incredibly free, wild, and natural about being naked. It's exhilarating and a bit rebellious.

Give your baby a little time every day to be naked. (Be sure to schedule this diaper-free time carefully to avoid accidents.) She'll enjoy the freedom, and you'll get plenty of bare-butt photos that will embarrass her when she's a teenager.

Affirmation: I'll occasionally let my baby be au naturel.

TEAMWORK

The children always helped their mother to edit my books.

—*Mark Twain*

Children love to help their parents work. Giving kids a "job" is good for two reasons: It empowers them to take responsibility, and it lets them participate in the daily details of parents' lives. Even a very small child can make a contribution if you give him the chance. Evan used to push "return" on the computer to help me write my books.

Find some way your child can help you make lemonade, lick envelopes, or send a fax. He'll love it. You know what? You'll love it, too, because it's great to have your child on your team.

Affirmation: My baby and I are on the same team.

CHOICES

Families with babies and families without babies are sorry for each other.

—Edgar Watson Howe

As I near fifty, I've met more and more people who've chosen not to have children. They say, "I just don't have the patience," or "I wouldn't want so many demands," or "I work hard and I love my freedom—I don't want to worry about supporting a family."

On the one hand, I understand their position. Raising children is hard, time-consuming, and expensive. On the other hand, as a mother, I find it hard to imagine life without children. It would seem empty and meaningless (although undoubtedly quieter).

In fact, having children and remaining child-free are both legitimate choices. Both involve tradeoffs and rewards. Both deserve understanding and acceptance.

Affirmation: I'm happy with my choice.

PERFECTION

We want our children to have picture-perfect lives.
— *Harriet Hodgson*

All parents start out with the dream that their children will have perfect lives. Their children will never suffer bruises, endure disappointments, or face failure—at least not if they can help it.

Gradually, parents come to their senses. They accept—even embrace—the fact that perfection is a fantasy and not necessarily the goal. The healthiest families are those in which children are exposed to reality and given tools for coping with hard times.

It's better for your child to have a rich, full life—including the inevitable ups and downs—and to develop the strength to learn from whatever comes her way.

Affirmation: I'll give up my illusions of a perfect life for my child.

A DAY IN THE LIFE

Your neighbor, a mother of two, raises her eyebrows when you give your baby the cookie he's been screaming for. "Isn't he a little spoiled?" she asks rather smugly. What are you supposed to say to her unsolicited assessment of your parenting?

Here's what you say: "It's really up to me to be the judge of that."

Of course, she may be right, even though her delivery is bound to make you angry. If you can get beyond your defensiveness, you may want to consider her comment, deciding for yourself if her point is valid.

Right or wrong, you needn't put up with anyone's harsh judgments. Frankly, whether you give your child the cookie is none of her business; she wouldn't like it if you made smug comments about her parenting decisions.

Like any mother, you make the best decisions you can, and the last thing you need is harsh criticism. What you need is support for being the best mother you know how to be.

Affirmation: Mothers need support, not criticism.

VALUES

*Parents owe their children a set of decent
standards and solid moral values around which
to build a life.*

—Ann Landers

Which of course begs the question: What are
decent standards? Your values and beliefs
constantly evolve. What you believe at twenty
is different from what you believe at thirty
and forty; having a child changes your beliefs
even more.

It's never too early to evaluate your beliefs and
determine how you can best pass them on to your
child. If you're overwhelmed by this prospect,
here's an interesting finding from experts in
child development: Kids who avoid the worst
problems—drug abuse, teen pregnancy, and the
like—were often taught values, regardless of what
those values were.

**Affirmation: My values are the right ones to
teach my child.**

TELEVISION

TV: The Third Parent.

—*R. Buckminster Fuller*

Your baby may not pay much attention to the television now, but it's never too early to think about the role TV will play in your child's life. How much TV should your child watch? What kind of programming is appropriate and what should you censor? Is violence really a problem? Should you use television as a baby sitter? As a reward?

Television is a constant presence. Hundreds of channels are available on satellite and cable, and thousands of movies are available on VHS and DVD. Some parents welcome television as an educational tool and a great way to get a break. Others perceive TV as an insidious competitor to other, more worthwhile family activities.

Wherever you fall in the spectrum, here's an experiment to try: For the next two or three days, turn off the television and see what happens. You'll probably find yourself choosing more discriminately when to turn it back on.

Affirmation: I'll monitor what and how much TV my child watches.

QUALITY TIME

The best inheritance a parent can give his child is a few minutes of time each day.

—*O. A. Battista*

Whether it's a few minutes or an entire evening, what matters most is how you spend time with your child. Is it really quality time—time spent attending to her, undistracted, without a million other thoughts shooting through your brain? Or is your attention elsewhere? Do you half-listen to your child while you're folding laundry, answering the phone, trying to get dinner on the table, or thinking about tomorrow's business meeting? You have so much to do. It's hard to stop everything and just be with your child. Yet what could possibly be more important? The time you spend with your child is invaluable—be sure to give her your undivided attention. It's the best gift of all.

Affirmation: I'll spend quality time with my child today.

CRITICISM

*Do not join encounter groups. If you enjoy being
made to feel inadequate, call your mother.*
—Liz Smith

At first I found this quote terribly insulting.
How dare humorist Liz Smith even facetiously
imply that mothers make their children feel bad
about themselves?

After calming down, I decided there's some
truth to what she says. Not out of malice, not
out of meanness, mothers do tend to criticize
their children. Mothers have such high hopes
and are so sensitive to their children's flaws.
Their well-meaning advice often focuses on the
negatives and overlooks the positives. This makes
children feel as if they can't possibly please their
mothers enough.

It isn't your child's job to make you happy.
Beginning today, commit to accept and affirm
your child's efforts and focus on the positives,
even when he falls short of your expectations.

**Affirmation: I'll watch my tendency to criticize
my child.**

PREPARATION

Be prepared.

—Girl Scouts motto

This could just as easily be the Mothers Motto.

Always be prepared for your baby to fall asleep right as you get into the car. Always be prepared for your child to spit up all over your shirt the minute you walk into the grocery store. Always be prepared for your child to catch a bad cold during the busiest time of the year.

Always be prepared with extra pacifiers, Band-Aids, a list of backup sitters, and all the spare patience you can muster. In case of an emergency —and there will be plenty—being prepared to regroup, revise, and improvise can make the difference between panic and peace of mind.

Affirmation: I'll always be prepared.

EATING OUT

Children never want to eat in restaurants. What they want is to play under the table until the entrées arrive, then go to the bathroom.
—Dave Barry

Your child might sit quietly in a highchair while you enjoy a lovely dinner out. More likely, she will cry, fill her diapers, and create a scene while your food gets cold.

Once your child gets older, it unfortunately won't get any better. You'll go off on expeditions to the bathroom and beg her to stop making sugar-and-ketchup concoctions.

I can count the times I've successfully managed eating out with kids. To be exact, three: once when the restaurant had a game room; once when a particularly nice waiter took the children for a tour of the kitchen; and once when a woman had a stroke and the paramedics came, which, heartless though it sounds, kept the kids' rapt attention until dessert arrived.

Eat at home. It's cheaper and a lot less trouble. Besides, it makes going out—and leaving the baby with a sitter—that much more of a treat.

Affirmation: We'll eat at home.

INNER STRENGTH

A woman is like a teabag—you can't tell how strong she is until you put her in hot water.
—Nancy Reagan

And you really don't know a mother's strength until her child's hurt or in any sort of danger.

Just witness a mother whose child has fallen down at the park. One second she's calmly sitting on a bench, reading a magazine; the next second, she's flying across the park like the Bionic Woman on a life-and-death mission.

A mother's strength is amazing to behold, as you may already know firsthand. You stay up four nights in a row, not even fatigued as you nurse your sick child back to health. You fight like a lioness when someone threatens or treats your child unfairly. You find courage and fortitude you didn't even know you possessed when your child's in need.

But you needn't wait for a crisis to know the extent of your inner strength. You should claim it and celebrate it every day.

Affirmation: I'm incredibly strong.

KINDNESS

Let your children be more in awe of your kindness than your power.

—George Savile

Kindness has a magical effect on a child. And your kindness carries more weight than your power.

There are many situations when you can choose compassion over castigation. Instead of reprimanding your child for acting out, you can hold him in your arms and say, "I can see you need attention right now." Instead of yelling at or punishing your child for knocking over a cup, you can gently say, "You must feel awfully sad now that you have no more juice."

There's no need to rule with a heavy hand. Sometimes discipline is necessary, but your child will obey and respect you much more when he knows not how powerful you are but how powerful your kindness is.

Affirmation: I can parent with kindness.

SOLITUDE

A mother is someone who: looks forward to getting a root canal so she can sit quietly in one place.

—Beth Mende Conny

A root canal? Maybe not. But most new moms will go to considerable lengths for a few hours of uninterrupted peace and quiet.

Two women in southern California banked on it: They opened a camp for moms, a weekend getaway where harried mothers rest, relax, and are waited on hand and foot.

Every mother deserves such a break, but it's at best a wistful fantasy for most. The problem is, most moms don't have the money and time.

Still, there are affordable ways to find solitude. Go to a coffee shop. Take a drive in the country. Or call a sitter, lock yourself in your bedroom, and spend an hour alone just sitting by the window, losing yourself in a book.

You need it, and you've earned it!

Affirmation: I'll savor the rare moments of solitude.

CONSCIENCE

The principal goal of parenting is to teach our children to become their own parents.
—Wayne Dyer

Or in Freudian terms, to develop your child's superego—the inner voice that legislates right from wrong and guides her in making wise and responsible decisions. It's the voice that warns, "No, don't touch the stove—it's hot!" It's the voice that says, "If you tear up that book, you won't be able to look at it anymore." It's the voice that reminds, "If you're nice to people, they'll be nice in return."

As your child begins to experience firsthand the consequences of her actions, the "parental voice" gradually becomes internalized. Instead of hearing your voice, she'll hear her own.

Affirmation: I'll help my child develop a sense of right and wrong.

REJOICING

Rejoice with your family in the beautiful land of life.

—Albert Schweitzer

Beginning with the birth of your child, being a family offers abundant opportunities for rejoicing. Each birthday, each holiday, each time your child achieves another milestone is cause for celebration.

You needn't limit your festivities to standard holidays or life-cycle events. Some families create rituals all their own. For example, many years ago my friend Rhoda, her husband, and their two children initiated an annual ritual in which each family member shared positive achievements. I know another family who goes all out on May Day, complete with a basket exchange and a neighborhood parade.

Rejoicing together bonds you as a family and gives you plenty of laughter and joy.

Affirmation: There's so much to celebrate.

OUTINGS

A museum is a perfect opportunity to stroll a baby to sleep, it'll get you exercise, and you'll spend six to ten bucks on admission.
—Julian Orenstein

You may not be an art lover or a history buff, but museums are great places for you and your baby to visit when you need a change of pace. Exploring a museum is a wonderful way to expand your mind and engage your senses—it's just the type of experience most new mothers say they miss the most from their "old" life.

As an added bonus, your baby will enjoy a leisurely stroll in a lovely setting. It's often quieter (and cheaper) than a stroll through a mall and more stimulating than a walk around the neighborhood.

Next time you're in the mood for an outing with the baby, stop by your local museum. Contemplating artifacts and masterpieces while your baby is nestled in a stroller or a carrier reminds you that although motherhood somewhat limits your life, it also offers plenty of opportunities for growth.

Affirmation: Museums are good for my baby and me.

SECRETS

No one can keep a secret better than a child.
—Victor Hugo

Your baby is delighted when you let him in on "secrets." Take time to share a few secrets with him every day. Your baby won't understand what you're saying, but he'll love this special attention.

In a few years, you can share real secrets with him. My son, Evan, still talks about the time he and his father secretly painted the bathroom a beautiful shade of lavender while Zoe and I were in Florida.

Being on the "inside" makes your child feel important and trusted. It's a way to help develop his confidence and develop a magical, one-of-a-kind bond between mother and child.

Affirmation: I'll share secrets with my child.

NEGATIVITY

Our children will hate us too, y'know.
                                        —*John Lennon*

When Zoe was eighteen months old, she turned
to me in fury after being refused a cookie and
screamed, "I hate you!"

I didn't know whether to laugh or cry.

Your baby's developing a greater range of
emotions, and she has most likely learned to
express anger and frustration. Still, it's hard to
accept that the baby who lovingly wraps her
tiny finger around your own may someday cast
powerfully negative emotions—even hatred—in
your direction.

There are two ways to prepare yourself for
when this happens. One, remember that it
happens to most parents. You, too, might have
felt the same way toward your parents at times.
It didn't mean you stopped loving your parents.
It just meant you were upset. Two, remember that
your child's an individual. It's natural for her to
express negative emotions, but you don't cause
her feelings and you can't control them.

**Affirmation: Even when my child expresses nega-
tive emotions, we still love each other deeply.**

STRUGGLING

We give our children the privilege of struggling.
—*Mary Susan Miller*

You grit your teeth, watching your child learn
to walk. He falls down, gets hurt, and then gets
up again. You clench your fists in frustration,
watching your child trying to master a spoon. You
wish fervently you could somehow short-circuit
his struggle.

Yet it's the only way he can learn.

Think of your own struggles. The hardest
times often yield the greatest lessons. The same
is true for your child. Even though it's difficult,
sometimes he can only grow stronger the
hard way.

What you can do is be there for your child with
open, sympathetic arms and the reassurance that
you'll do everything in your power to help.

**Affirmation: Struggling teaches my child
inner strength.**

RESTROOMS

What it really means to be a parent is: you will spend an enormous portion of your time lurking outside public toilet stalls.

—Dave Barry

This may not be a savory subject, but let's take a minute to talk about kids and public restrooms.

The changing tables in women's restrooms in airports are terrific conveniences, but why aren't they also in the men's restrooms? What's a father traveling with an infant or toddler supposed to do? And how about women's facilities that don't allow boys over the age of two? Are moms supposed to let their young sons go into the men's room unattended while they wait nervously outside?

All parents need to lobby for family-friendly restrooms in their communities. Ask local businesses to adopt an innovation that I saw at the Mall of America near Minneapolis: family restrooms. Everyone's welcome, no discrimination allowed. It's nonsexist, and it's a lot safer.

Affirmation: Families deserve better restrooms.

PRESENT MOMENT

Children think not of what is past nor what is to come; they enjoy the present, which very few of us do.

—Jean de La Bruyère

Your baby lives life in the present. She doesn't mull over the past or fret about the future as most adults do. All her attention, emotions, and thoughts are focused on each moment as it happens. With adults, there's often a disconnection between what the body is doing and what the mind is thinking, which means adults often miss the little details that make life so amazing.

Learn from your baby's example. Set aside your regrets from yesterday. Set aside your worries about tomorrow. Allow yourself to fully engage in the present. You'll find that life is more profound, more exciting, more rewarding when you commit both your mind and body to the here and now.

Affirmation: I'll live in the present.

RATIONALIZATION

*Yes, having a child is surely the most beautifully
irrational act that two people in love can commit.*
—Bill Cosby

When your baby is sweetly sleeping in your arms,
you can admit that becoming a mother was the
wisest thing you've ever done. It's so good to
have meaning in your life and a beautiful child
to love.

But when you've been up forty-eight hours
with a screaming baby and a throbbing headache,
you can't help but think having a child was the
most irrational act you've ever committed. You
feel as if you were crazy—certifiably insane—to
take on such responsibility, to sacrifice so much.
What could you possibly have been thinking?

It's not a contradiction. Having a baby is the
wisest, most irrational, and best act of your life.

**Affirmation: Having a baby is the best thing I've
ever done.**

SPONTANEITY

Routines teach him security, while spontaneity will teach him to be open and creative to experience life in a fun-filled way.

—Becky Daniel

Close your eyes and think about something your baby has never done before. Better yet, think of something you've never done before with your baby. If you can, go do it—now.

As a mother, you need to provide routine and consistency so your baby feels secure. But you also need to instill in him a flair for spontaneity so he learns to appreciate the unexpected. Balancing the expected with the unexpected will develop your baby's zest for life, and it'll put some fun back into your life, too.

Affirmation: Spontaneity adds zest to life.

SEASONS

Sing a song of seasons!
Something bright in all!
                    —*Robert Louis Stevenson*

Each season is beautiful in its own way—it's especially true this year. This is the first time your baby will experience the wonder of spring, summer, fall, and winter.

Take your baby outdoors to explore each season. As long as the weather isn't too harsh and as long as your baby is dressed appropriately, each season is open for her enjoyment.

Perhaps the best time to take your baby out-doors is when the seasons are in transition, such as when the first fall frost clings to the morning grass as winter approaches or when the tiny, green buds on the trees tentatively open as spring gives way to summer.

Experiencing the cycle of the seasons will teach your baby that change is a beautiful part of life.

Affirmation: I'll help my baby enjoy the four seasons.

WHOLENESS

Women's work is always toward wholeness.
—May Sarton

Integration is another word for wholeness. The great challenge facing most mothers is integrating the various aspects of life—marriage, children, career, friendships, and physical, emotional, and spiritual fulfillment—into a working balance.

It's all too easy to neglect essential parts of yourself, especially when your child is small; his needs are too immediate (and often too loud) to ignore. So you focus on your child, putting the other aspects of your life on hold.

Days will grow into weeks, into months, into years of self-neglect unless you break the pattern right now and commit to putting all the pieces of your life back together.

Affirmation: All sides of my life deserve attention.

PRIVACY

The mother—poor invaded soul—finds even the bathroom door no bar to hammering little hands.
—*Charlotte Perkins Gilman*

As I complete this book, I've noticed that bathrooms pop up again and again on these pages. Maybe it's because mothers spend an awful lot of time in the bathroom, either keeping children company or escaping their company for a few blissful moments of peace.

Here are my final words on the subject: Lock the door. Unless your child is in danger (playpens and swings were invented so you can have bathroom breaks), you have every right to your privacy. Saying, "Right now, I get to be alone" is a basic example of setting limits.

Being a good mother doesn't mean being at your child's beck and call. If you get only one moment of privacy in your day, let it be this.

Affirmation: I'll preserve the most basic privacy of all.

EMPOWERMENT

Even a two-year-old can be asked whether he
wants half a glass of milk or a full glass of milk.
                                        —Haim G. Ginott

Too often, you make decisions for your child
without asking for her input. You assume her
opinion wouldn't make a difference because
choosing milk from juice or a sweater from a
jacket is trivial. Or perhaps you think asking for
her opinion is ridiculous, since she can't even talk.

Of course, your child isn't ready to make all or
even many of her own decisions. But by asking
every now and then for your child's input—even
if she can't yet talk—you show her respect. You
cultivate her sense of responsibility. You help build
her confidence so she can make bigger decisions
as she grows.

Affirmation: I'll solicit my child's input.

WORRIES

I used to be a reasonably adventurous person before I had children; now I am constantly afraid that a low flying aircraft will drop on my children's school.

—Margaret Drabble

You can worry yourself sick imagining all the terrible things that can happen to your child. What if he gets some terrible illness? What if something happens to your or your partner's career, and there's not enough money to support the family? What if your child is kidnapped? What if? What if? What if?

The world is dangerous, and awful things do happen. But you can't stop living because of fear. Rather, you need to cultivate faith—faith that you'll have the courage to meet life's challenges and steer your child through any storm.

Affirmation: I'll focus on what I can control, not on what I can't control.

NEGATIVITY

To think is to say no.

—*Alain*

Sometimes you wonder if this is your child's personal philosophy. The instant your baby learns the word *no*, she seems to forget all other words. She even says no when she really means yes! It's enough to drive you crazy.

This is certainly a difficult phase to cope with, but take some comfort in the fact that it's a necessary developmental phase. When your baby says no, she displays independent thinking. She's learning how to think for herself, formulate an opinion, and then communicate that opinion.

Unfortunately, your baby isn't capable of forming many opinions beyond "no" at this time. It doesn't mean she's destined to have a pessimistic personality. And no matter how much you'd like to believe it, it doesn't mean she's trying to send you to the loony bin.

Affirmation: My baby learns to think for herself by saying no.

PMS

Women complain about premenstrual syndrome, but I think of it as the only time of the month I can be myself.

—Roseanne

If you experience PMS, that time of the month presents an extra mothering challenge.

How can you be patient with your child when you're crabby and out of sorts? How can you control outbursts and keep things in perspective? How can you stay focused on all your responsibilities when you feel like crawling into bed and hiding under the covers?

These are the times when you need to go easy on yourself. Or when you need to take some extra time off. You need to remember that being a good mother doesn't mean you have to be cheerful, even-tempered, and sweet every day of the month.

Affirmation: I'll go easy on myself when it's that time of the month.

DISCIPLINE

Just wait until your father comes home!
                                    —Countless mothers

Many adults heard this threat while growing up.
Mothers abdicated sole responsibility for discipline
to fathers. The result? Kids were afraid of their
fathers, and they didn't take their mothers
very seriously.

You and your partner may already know who's
the "good cop" and who's the "bad cop." Even
your baby may know which parent can be tested
and which means business. One of you (and it's
not just fathers anymore) may be firmer than the
other when telling the baby no or when removing
him from trouble.

If you believe in equal parenting, you must
share both the tender and the tough parts of
parenting. This means both of you need to be
serious when disciplining your child.

Affirmation: We'll share the duty of discipline.

REASSURANCE

Piglet sidled up to Pooh from behind.

"Pooh," he whispered.

"Yes, Piglet?"

"Nothing," said Piglet, taking Pooh's paw, "I just wanted to be sure of you."

—*A. A. Milne*

Sometimes your child needs a little bit of reassurance. Her fingers wrap around you, simply wanting to feel your bigger hand encircling her own. She follows you from room to room, keeping track of your whereabouts. She cries in the middle of the night just to make sure you're right where she can find you.

What does your baby want? Nothing in particular yet everything your presence represents: security, comfort, love.

Affirmation: Baby, I'm right here.

MORNINGS

The trouble with dawn is that it comes too early in the day.

—Susan Richman

It comes way too early and way too often, especially when your child is small.

For those who cherish their sleep (count me in), early mornings heralded by a child's voice or cry (usually eager and way too loud) are tough. Every little bit of sleep is a gift from God; you roll over and pray for another few minutes of blissful slumber before facing the day.

Some mothers actually grow to enjoy sunrise, while others say they never get used to its glare. In either case, here are the two best pieces of advice I've heard on the subject: Don't check the clock to calculate how long you've rested, and wait fifteen minutes before deciding how you feel.

Affirmation: I can survive these early mornings.

TOYS

Toys are made in heaven, batteries are made in hell.

—Tom Robbins

Those darn battery-operated toys. Inevitably, children unwrap birthday or holiday gifts only to discover they're missing the batteries. The parents are off to the store faster than you can say "Energizer," coming home only to find the toys need AAs—not the AAAs they bought.

Then there are toys that require assembly. Parents spend hours on their hands and knees, putting pieces together. Finally, there are noisy toys that leave parents with splitting headaches.

So when you buy toys for your child now and in the years to come, consider how much you yourself will like them. You may find yourself shopping for books and blocks and other toys that don't require batteries, don't need to be assembled, and don't make noise.

Affirmation: I'll buy toys that are "kid-tested, mother-approved."

A DAY IN THE LIFE

Looking through your own baby record book, you discover that you were toilet trained before your first birthday—roughly at the age your baby is now. Does this mean you can start toilet training and say good-bye to diapers forever?

Most likely not. Despite evidence that some children have been toilet trained before their first birthdays, most experts agree that training is most successful when children are between ages two and three.

If you want to get a head start on the process, help your child understand what happens when he urinates or has a bowel movement. If he realizes what it means to go "potty" in his diaper now, it'll be easier to convince him to do the same in a toilet later on.

So don't throw out the diapers just yet. You may be eager to toilet train your baby, but a calm, patient attitude is what's needed here. The less you force it, the greater your chances of success. When he's ready, he'll give up diapers.

Affirmation: I won't rush toilet training.

AFFECTION

*My mother was raised with a terror of touching,
which left me feeling needy.*
—Mariette Hartley

One of my favorite bumper stickers is the one that
reads, "Have You Hugged Your Child Today?"

It always makes me think, have I hugged my
children today? Did I kiss them and cuddle them
and ruffle their hair, or was I so busy and distracted that a day went by without expressing
my love?

Your child's very receptive to your affection
when she's small. She craves it. She welcomes it.
It makes her feel secure and loved.

As she grows older, she'll be less open to your
physical affection, though she'll still come around
for a cuddle every now and then. This makes it
terribly important to hug and cuddle and hold
your child a lot now, when she needs it like water
and air.

Affirmation: I'll hug my child today.

PRIORITIES

Having it all doesn't necessarily mean having it all at once.

—Stephanie Luetkehans

You've likely figured this one out by now: When you have a child, you need to table some of your other goals and ambitions, if only to preserve your energy and maintain your sanity.

But here's a guideline: The tradeoffs you make must be consistent with your most deeply held values. If you get complete satisfaction from caring for your baby and the household, you might remain at home and sacrifice your career. If your job gives you a sense of accomplishment and fulfillment, you might return to your career but sacrifice time with the baby.

Your values will change over time. What's important is that you seriously evaluate and be at peace with your values and choices today.

Affirmation: I know what matters most to me.

PEACEKEEPING

Parents are not interested in justice, they are interested in quiet.

—Bill Cosby

Being a mother is a lot like being a referee. Whether you have several children of your own or one child with playmates, you're constantly called upon to arbitrate. And whatever call you make, somebody will read you the riot act.

Veteran moms offer this advice: Stay on the sidelines as much as possible. Whether it's figuring out whose turn it is with the ball or mediating sibling-rivalry battles, the best call is to encourage kids—even babies—to work it out themselves. The more kids negotiate with one another, the better they get at learning to solve problems on their own.

Affirmation: I'll try to stand on the sidelines.

LIFE ROLES

When people ask me what I do, I always say I am a mother first.

—Jacqueline Jackson

You can be a career woman, a lover, a daughter, a friend—but once you have a child, you're always a mother first.

Sometimes this label leads to deep conflict. When your newborn's under the weather, you feel guilty going out for supper with your partner and leaving the baby with a sitter. When you have lunch with friends, you're preoccupied because you wonder how much rice cereal your baby's eating at home. When you miss your baby's first steps because you were at work, you have trouble forgiving yourself, even though it couldn't have been avoided.

You'll always be a mother first, but you need to let go and accept that the other roles in your life are important, too. Being a complete woman makes you a better mother.

Affirmation: I'm always a mother, but I'm other things, too.

FAMILY VACATIONS

There's no such thing as "fun for the whole family."
—Jerry Seinfeld

Family vacations seem wonderful, especially when you're planning them and when you're back home reminiscing over the photographs.

In between the planning and the reminiscing, family vacations often fall short of your fantasies. Why? Because a vacation with a baby simply isn't a vacation. You lug around diaper bags and car seats and other baby paraphernalia. You get very little rest because the baby doesn't sleep well in a hotel crib or in your bed. You struggle to maintain the baby's napping and feeding schedule, leaving little time to see the sights or otherwise enjoy your vacation. All too often, you return home more exhausted than when you left.

Unless you're going to a family resort with round-the-clock child care or bringing a nanny, it's best to keep expectations realistic. Vacationing with your baby isn't an opportunity for rest and relaxation. Rather, it's a way of making memories that your family will look back on and treasure.

Affirmation: I'll rest when I get home.

NOISE

When my kids become wild and unruly, I use a nice, safe playpen. When they're finished, I climb out.

—Erma Bombeck

Have you ever noticed how parents of grown children talk about how quiet it is once their kids leave home?

Children can be noisy, wild, and unruly. They're spirited, and thank goodness. You'd worry if your child sat passively in a corner. Notice, for example, how thrilled and relieved you are when your child recovers from being ill and resumes making his usual ruckus.

You become inured to the clatter, yet sometimes it takes its toll, leaving you crabby and frustrated. Sometimes you need to escape from the din. You need to take a short break or insist on mandatory quiet time—for your child and for you—until you're ready to cope with his seemingly boundless energy.

Affirmation: I'm grateful for my child's energy— someday I'll miss the clatter.

A DAY IN THE LIFE

Your daughter sleeps through the night, you've lost the weight you gained in pregnancy, and you and your husband have resumed your usual romantic relationship. So everything's perfect… except for the tiny voice in your head that keeps saying, "Time to have another baby."

Unless you're certain that you want only one child, the "When should we get pregnant again?" question typically comes up right around the first birthday, just when life seems to be finally settling down.

Some people argue that when you're in baby mode, you may as well not waste time having another. And there's something to be said for siblings close in age; they can share toys and look after each other once they're in school.

But then there's the "diaper dilemma." Many parents wait until the older child is out of diapers. Plus, experts agree that sibling rivalry is diminished with a few years between the children.

Whether sooner or later, a second child creates both upheaval and joy.

Affirmation: Having a baby is just as big a decision the second time around.

PRAISE

I praise loudly; I blame softly.

—*Catherine II*

Excellent advice, but too often you do exactly the opposite. You forget to praise your child in front of others, taking his good behavior for granted. Instead, you reprimand your child when he falls short of the mark so you can show others that you're a good mother who corrects misbehavior.

Shouting "Great job!" loud enough for all to hear tells your child that you're proud of his efforts. Taking your child aside and whispering, "This isn't the way to behave" tells him what you expect without robbing him of his dignity.

Affirmation: I'll praise loudly, reprimand softly.

WISDOM

Wisdom is knowing when you can't be wise.
—Paul Engle

As you gain experience as a parent, you also gain wisdom—the wisdom that tells you just how much you really don't know, just how much is really involved in being a good parent. It takes this wisdom and humility to recognize when you need help.

During those times, it's important to seek support and assistance from your pediatrician, a child-development counselor, other professionals, or other parents who can share their experiences and guide you.

You needn't ever be ashamed or embarrassed to ask for help. The wisdom to acknowledge your limits and the willingness to stretch them are all you need to grow wise as a parent.

Affirmation: I'm strong enough to ask for help.

ROMANCE

For me, motherhood has been the one true, great, and wholly successful romance.

—Erma Kurtz

In some ways, your devotion to your child transcends all other human connection; no one seems to have more power than your child to make your heart heavy with sorrow, weightless with joy.

At times it can seem as if your feelings for your child are stronger, more intimate than your feelings for your partner. But remember that your love for your child and your love for your partner are both vastly important.

You must always make time to nurture your romance with the one person you chose to share your life with, the one person you chose to create a beautiful child with, and the one person you chose to grow old with.

Affirmation: I'll kindle the fires of my relationship with my partner.

A DAY IN THE LIFE

Your best friend just came over to tell you she's pregnant. She asks you what it's really like to be a mom. Speaking as the voice of experience, what do you say?

Do you tell her that so far it's been the greatest adventure of your life? Do you talk about how hard it is and how much work it involves? Can you possibly convey the intense mixture of love, fear, pride, vulnerability, apprehension, and excitement you've experienced and will continue to experience as a mother?

Even if no one has asked you this specific question, this is a good opportunity to stop and take stock. Reflect on the past year. What were the highlights? The low points? What strengths have you gained? What wisdom? What gifts?

Ask yourself this question: "What is it like to be a mother?"

Affirmation: Being a mother is _____

_____.

MEANING

Being a mother is what I think has made me the person I am.

—Jacqueline Kennedy Onassis

These words come from an incredible woman whose life experiences included being a First Lady, wife of a billionaire, world citizen, and successful book editor. Yet what did the late Jackie O. consider her most significant, life-shaping experience? Motherhood.

I'm not surprised. No matter what else you achieve, being a mother shapes your character more than anything else will. The lessons you learn in motherhood—patience, understanding, compassion, gratitude, and forgiveness—profoundly affect who you are and how you carry yourself in every other sphere of your life.

Affirmation: I'm forever changed by the experience of motherhood.

EFFORT

Nine years later, I can still remember my first baby's first birthday in every detail. Naturally, I overdid it.

—*Vicki Iovine*

As you approach your baby's first birthday, you may be planning a party. If so, here's something to consider:

For one of Evan's birthday parties, I spent an hour and a half cutting crusts off twenty-four slices of Wonder Bread for peanut-butter-and-jelly sandwiches. At one of Zoe's parties, I labored over decorating rice cakes as clowns, with shredded-carrot hair, raisin eyes, and gumdrop noses.

Over the years, I calmed down considerably. Some parties featured takeout pizza. One year I really wised up and invited the guests to come at three in the afternoon, so I got away with serving just cupcakes and milk.

Did the guests care? Of course not. Did I? Not after I realized that being a good mother doesn't require such Martha Stewart–ish efforts. Sometimes simpler is better.

Affirmation: I don't have to go to extreme lengths to be a good mother.

NURTURING

I felt about my children as if they were plants.
—Jehan Sadat

Like a plant, your child needs light and water, love and gentle tending in order to flourish.

You enlighten her through education and example. You nourish her with healthy food and a nurturing environment. You gently tend to her spirit by giving her love, consistent guidance, and perennial devotion.

Then you watch with pride as she blossoms.

Affirmation: My child is like a beautiful plant; I'll nurture her so she can blossom.

TOGETHERNESS

Grow up together, constantly.

—Leo Buscaglia

This is a perfect blessing for parents and children. Parenting involves constant growth, not only for children but for parents as well.

But for your family to "grow up" together, you need to be open to learning, you need to have fun, and you need always to appreciate the strength of your love.

So here's what I'd add to Leo Buscaglia's blessing:

Learn together, constantly.

Laugh together, constantly.

Love together, constantly.

Doing so makes you a family. Together, you learn and laugh and love and grow.

Affirmation: It's a blessing to grow as a family.

DREAMS

Every mother has a secret dream for her child.
—*Louise DeGrave*

Your hopes and dreams for your child evolved
as you made the transition from pregnancy to
childbirth to motherhood.

Now that you know your child, now that he's
a person you can see and touch and feel, what
are your secret hopes and dreams for him? Do
you dream your child will be a loving and kind
person? Do you dream of him coming of age
in a secure and peaceful world? Do you dream
of him someday having his own child and
experiencing the joys of parenthood?

Every mother has her own dreams. What
are yours?

Affirmation: My dream for my child is _____
_____.

GUIDANCE

*My responsibility is to provide them a map, a
lunch for the way and salve for bear scratches.*
                                   —Ellen Walker

You provide your child the signposts to help her
travel life's journey safely and happily. You teach
her values, skills, and right from wrong.

   You provide necessary equipment. Today, you
put a pacifier in her diaper bag, tomorrow you'll
put an eraser in her pencil box, and the next day
you'll put change in her pocket to call home when
she ventures out on her own.

   And you'll always be ready with salve and
soothing words for the inevitable hurts she'll
endure along the journey.

   Ultimately, this is what mothering comes down
to, no matter where your child goes or how old
she gets.

Affirmation: I'll help my child travel life's journey.

INTENSITY

Being a mother is rewarding to one's female instincts, trying to one's nerves, physically exhausting, emotionally both frustrating and satisfying, and, above all, not to be undertaken lightly.

—Margaret Raphael

Motherhood is the most universal experience women share. Yet if you ask a hundred women what it's really like to be a mother, you're likely to hear a hundred different—and seemingly contradictory—descriptions.

"Being a mom is exciting," says one woman. "It's incredibly boring and monotonous," says another. One says, "It's the easiest, most natural thing in the world." Another replies, "It's the single hardest thing I've ever done."

Yet through all these descriptions runs a common thread: intensity. Whether mothers talk about anticipation or apprehension, hopes or fears, bliss or sorrow, most women say motherhood is a profound, emotional, and intense experience.

Allow yourself to feel that intensity. It's an integral part of what makes you a mother.

Affirmation: Motherhood is an intense experience.

PRAYER

Pray to God. She will help you.
—*Alva Vanderbilt-Belmont*

When all else fails, there's always the power of prayer to help you through the ongoing struggles and challenges of motherhood.

Prayer—however you define it—comforts and strengthens you. As the Jewish saying goes, "All prayer is longing." It's longing for guidance, longing for courage, longing for the wisdom to give your child what he needs.

Yet prayer is also a way of giving thanks. As you look at your child, there's so very, very much to be grateful for.

Affirmation: I offer prayers of longing and gratitude.

LOVE

A mother is someone who loves you.

—Evan Stern

I leave you with these simple words my son said when he was eight.

"But why does she love you?" I pressed Evan. His answer: "Because you're her only eight-year-old son."

What more is there to say? When you get right down to it, you don't love your child because she's cute or smart or well-behaved. You love her just because she's your child and because you have the great privilege of being her mother.

You love her fiercely. You love her completely. You love her forever.

Affirmation: I love you because I'm your mother and you're my child.

Also from Meadowbrook Press

✦ **_Reflections for Newlyweds_**
The 365 daily reflections in this book nurture a couple through the ups, downs, and in-betweens along the journey of love. Designed for newlyweds to read together, this book will open lines of fruitful communication and help build a strong relationship.

✦ **_Reflections for Expectant Mothers_**
This inspirational book guides the expectant mother through all the miracles that mark the transition to motherhood. The 40 weeks of daily reflections offer words of encouragement from such sources as Anna Quindlen, Roseanne Barr, and Dorothy Parker.

We offer many more titles written to delight, inform, and entertain.
To order books with a credit card or browse our full
selection of titles, visit our web site at:

www.meadowbrookpress.com

or call toll-free to place an order, request a free catalog, or ask a question:

1-800-338-2232

Meadowbrook Press • 5451 Smetana Drive • Minnetonka, MN • 55343